100 YEARS BOLD

100 YEARS BOLD

1913–2013

THE CENTENNIAL HISTORY OF BOSTON UNIVERSITY SCHOOL OF MANAGEMENT

JAMES E. POST

Boston University School of Management

595 Commonwealth Avenue

Boston, MA 02215

www.management.bu.edu

Published in cooperation with

Reedy Press

PO Box 5131

St. Louis, MO 63139

www.reedypress.com

Library of Congress Control Number: on file

ISBN: 978-1-935806-58-5

Cover design by Margaret M. Price

Interior design by Nick Hoeing

Printed in the United States of America

13 14 15 16 17   1 2 3 4 5

CONTENTS

The atrium lobby in the Rafik B. Hariri Building is a hub of student and community activity, 2013

DEAN'S LETTER

Upon joining Boston University School of Management as the Allen Questrom Professor and Dean, I had high expectations. Looking back three years later, they have been surpassed.

There is nothing that rivals the privilege of serving the next generation of global leaders, engaging talented young men and women inside and outside the classroom as they discover who they are, and prepare to live responsible professional and personal lives. Remarkably, the School of Management has been exercising this privilege for one hundred years in practical, progressive, and effective ways. The world has changed dramatically along the way, and so has the School.

This is our proud story, marked by a number of events that have defined who we are, and where we are heading. We extend our deep gratitude to James E. Post, the John F. Smith, Jr. Professor in Management, for the care with which he has compiled our history, grounded in thirty-nine years of experience on the School's faculty and his meticulous scholarly approach.

CONGRATULATIONS to our almost 50,000 alumni, faculty, and staff that have together completed the first chapter, the first one hundred years, in Boston University School of Management's rise to a position among the world's elite business schools.

—Kenneth W. Freeman,
Allen Questrom Professor and Dean

INTRODUCTION

Today, Boston University School of Management (SMG) is home to more than 3,400 students (2,200 undergraduates and 1,200 graduate students) and nearly 50,000 alumni. This book tells the story of the school's evolution, tracing its history and highlighting some of the many ways SMG has created value for one hundred years. It is the story of a community—visionary leaders, dedicated faculty and staff, enthusiastic students, and generous benefactors—who, together, have created one of the world's premier business schools.

The year 2013 marks the centennial anniversary of Boston University School of Management. Founded as the College of Business Administration (CBA), the school opened as an evening program in 1913, introduced a full-time undergraduate degree program in 1916, and launched a master's program in 1917. The first undergraduate class graduated in 1917, and from there, CBA gathered steam. In 1974, the college was renamed "School of Management," reflecting its evolving goal to help shape well-trained, effective managers for business, government, and nonprofit institutions.

The story of SMG's development has many currents—and crosscurrents—running beneath the surface. As a river flows in one direction, its currents and crosscurrents typically move at different rates, speeds, and depths. Such is the case with academic life as well.

One theme of this story involves leadership and the ambitions of founders, deans, and faculty who charted the school's course over a century. A second theme involves the evolution of core values and the mission to which the school is committed, ranging from the notion of "service to society" to "creating value for the world." Yet a third theme involves the experience of students: the social organizations each generation built, through memorable relationships, study groups, and teams. There are families and friends, significant events, high points and low points, all entwined in one educational experience.

This book attempts to connect these facts, experiences, and relationships, and to communicate them as a coherent story. Inevitably, this version will differ from the recollections of any individual student, faculty, or staff member. No one has experienced every crosscurrent of the story, nor have their experiences exactly matched those of their peers. Still, the hope is that everyone will relate to various aspects of the story, while also learning something new as they read this account of SMG's "river of time."

There is no other book that explains the story of Boston University School of Management, but there are several invaluable resources for those interested in the school's history. Eleanor Rust Collier prepared a helpful paper describing the College of Business Administration from 1913 to 1959; the unpublished paper is housed in the university's Howard Gotlieb Archival Research Center.[1] The university's sesquicentennial volume, *Transformations: A History of Boston University*, published in 1991,[2] places the story of the business school in the larger institutional context of Boston University history. But it sheds little light on the people, programs, and decisions that shaped the business school in those early decades, and contains nothing about the past twenty-five years, a time of

extraordinary and transformative change at the School of Management. *100 Years Bold* draws on these sources and upon a host of facts, stories, and recollections of faculty, administrators, deans, and students. The result is a coherent view of how SMG was formed, developed, and evolved into today's Boston University School of Management.

I have lived through many interesting changes during four decades at SMG. But when I began studying the life of founding dean, Everett W. Lord, I realized how little was known about the early history of the school and the challenges it overcame from the 1920s to the 1970s. With the help of colleagues, I began to piece together the story of a university that reluctantly started a business program as a means of attracting more men to campus. When it succeeded, university leaders quickly embraced it and endorsed Dean Lord's remarkable leadership. Indeed, when he retired in 1941, the university's press release said, "Whatever the college is today, he made it."

The history of the school, as I see it, involves four turning points: the decision to open the Day Division in 1916, the building of the Charles Hayden Memorial as CBA's home in 1939, the renaming of CBA as the School of Management in 1974, and the building of the School's current home at 595 Commonwealth Avenue in the mid-1990s during Dean Louis E. Lataif's tenure. Readers may wonder whether the School is at another turning point today, as Kenneth W. Freeman, the current Allen Questrom Professor and Dean, leads the school toward even greater public recognition and global reach.

As Boston University School of Management begins its second century, I hope that this account will foster appropriate pride in our community's accomplishments. Ideally, it will also inspire new generations to advance the school's sense of purpose: from the founder's vision of "service to society" to today's vision of "creating value for the world" with boldness and imagination.

I have written many books throughout my career, but few have been as enjoyable as this centennial project. I hope that readers also enjoy this inspiring story of achievement, improvement, and impact.

—James E. Post, JD, PhD
John F. Smith, Jr. Professor in Management

NOTES

1. Elizabeth Rust Collier, "Boston University, College of Business Administration, 1913-1958" (unpublished paper, Boston University Archives, 1959).
2. Kathleen Kilgore, *Transformations* (Boston: Boston University, 1991).

100 YEARS BOLD

CHAPTER ONE
THE FOUNDING

A "Mad, Modernist Moment"

The year 1913 was a year of shocking social change and momentous events in the United States and Europe.

These events revolutionized what Dean Everett W. Lord described as both the "cultural" and the "practical" sides of life. In the opinion of the man who would shape Boston University's College of Business Administration for decades to come, the educated person to whom leadership responsibilities could be entrusted must be well versed in each of these spheres. In 1913, Americans were being swept up in turbulent changes across both arenas.

"A MAD, MODERNIST MOMENT"

The revolutionary changes taking place in American and European culture were so fundamental that they would ripple across the entire twentieth century. In Vienna, the audience at a concert of new, modern music by Schoenberg broke out in a near riot. At an exhibition in a New York armory, American viewers stood confounded before cubist and abstract paintings. "And in Paris, Stravinsky and Nijinsky's new ballet, *The Rite of Spring*, burst on stage with inflammatory results."[1] Looking back, 1913 was, in the words of one reviewer, "a mad, Modernist moment."

On the practical side of life, economic changes were also occurring that would bring lasting social and political consequences. Henry Ford introduced the first moving assembly line in 1913; its long rows of felt-capped workers hunched over streams of moving parts reduced the chassis automobile assembly time from 12.5 hours per car to 2 hours, 40 minutes (720 minutes to 160 minutes). The assembly line demonstrated the power of integrating men and machines in what came to be called the era of "scientific management." On December 23, President Woodrow Wilson signed the Owen-Glass Act creating the Federal Reserve Bank system—the first major banking reform since the Civil War, intended to regulate banks and create a more stable monetary system in the aftermath of the Panic of 1907. The twelve regional banks of the Federal Reserve Bank system would begin operating in 1914. American business was about to be transformed.

Momentous political changes were also taking place. On March 4, 1913, Woodrow Wilson was inaugurated as the twenty-eighth president of the United States. One month before Wilson's inauguration, the Sixteenth Amendment to the U.S. Constitution was ratified, allowing Congress to levy an income tax without apportioning it among the states or basing it on census results. This amendment permitted individual and corporate income taxes to be levied, thus launching the modern progressive tax system. The Seventeenth Amendment was ratified on June 11, allowing for the direct election of Senators by citizens rather than election by state legislators. Each of these developments would impact our nation's very notions of citizenship, community, and leadership.

THE EARLY YEARS

Later that same year, on an early fall evening, business education at Boston University began. It was Monday, October 13, 1913, and several dozen students gathered to take classes in English, Spanish, and advertising. On subsequent evenings, they attended classes on business organization, accounting, and finance. The curriculum, though perhaps a surprising mix to today's managers, reflected Dean Lord's belief in the importance of both the cultural and the practical.

As Kathleen Kilgore, author of Boston University's sesquicentennial history volume,

Transformations, observed, "The history of institutions begins with stories of individuals."[2] The Boston University School of Management was shaped by people whose stories remain vital. Over the course of a century, hundreds of talented faculty members have taught thousands of energetic students. At the helm stood a succession of leaders—deans, assistant deans, associate deans, department chairs— and a handful of BU presidents whose visions of the modern university fostered the creation of a first-rate school of management.

The school has benefited from deans who built an enterprise that now ranks among the finest business education institutions in the world. Those leaders often shared visions that required the support of the university's president and trustees. But the school's history did not unfold without its own management challenges.

One struggle involved efforts of the deans to manage expectations and persuade a sitting president of the wisdom of a particular course of action. Dean Lord often used his annual reports to urge presidents Lemuel Murlin (1911–24) and Daniel Marsh (1926–51) to assign the school more physical space to grow; Dean Peter Gabriel famously clashed with President

Everett W. Lord, circa 1913, founding dean of College of Business Administration

John Silber about strategic direction in the 1970s; and, nearly every dean has lamented being unable to persuade presidents to address financial and facilities issues.

The story of CBA/SMG also involves many unexpected twists. The school's fortunes have risen and fallen over the decades, affected by a kaleidoscope of people, institutional issues, and economic, social, and political events. At each identifiable turning point, bold decisions were made, dramatically shaping the trajectory of the school's development.

TURNING POINT #1: CREATING A SENSE OF PURPOSE

At its heart, the CBA/SMG story pivots around the decisions made at four critical turning points. The first occurred in the early years of the school's existence and arose from a particularly difficult management challenge: the very idea of starting a business school was dismissed, at least at first, by BU's leaders.

An "Impractical, Extravagant, Undesirable" Proposal

In 1912, alumnus Everett W. Lord proposed the teaching of business courses in the College of Liberal Arts (CLA) as a way to attract more men as students. University leaders immediately shot down the idea. President Lemuel Murlin circulated Lord's proposal to the faculty of College of Liberal Arts, who described it variously as "Impractical. Contrary to the principles of Boston University. Extravagant. Unacademic, unbusinesslike," and even, to their apparent horror, "visionary." In a word: "undesirable."

But, as in any good story of rivalry, the CLA faculty also had an economic motive for opposing the proposal. CLA was running a deficit, and the faculty feared their students would switch to business classes. From the president's perspective, it seemed pointless to hire faculty without a guarantee of increased enrollment.

Lord and his band of local organizers held their ground, though, and eventually negotiated a

President Lemuel Murlin, circa 1913

compromise: the college could begin operations if sufficient funding was raised from outside sources to cover the risk. Murlin, both agreeing reluctantly and drawing his own line in the sand, cautioned, "This will place the proposed school under no financial pressure, which might tempt, or might be considered likely to tempt, the school to maintain low standards."[3] In response, Lord revised his original proposal to recommend the creation of a separate college of business administration with guaranteed financial support from the business community. It was a bold plan.

GAMBLING ON SUCCESS

Lord moved to organize a group of guarantors to purchase $10,000 of bonds that would guarantee funding for three years. The first bonds he sold were to the governor and to Boston's mayor, John F. ("Honey Fitz") Fitzgerald. But the first real glimmer of hope came from out of nowhere: a contractor named Hugh Nawn, whom Lord barely knew, agreed to buy $500 of bonds. "Sure, it sounds like a good thing," Nawn remarked offhandedly. "I wish I'd had such a chance."[4]

With funding in hand, Boston University offered its first business courses in the fall term of 1913. In his first annual report to President Murlin, Dean Lord wrote: "Sir: I have the honor to submit the first annual report of the College of Business Administration, covering the past academic year, from October 13, 1913 to May 22, 1914. During this period, the College was in session thirty weeks, divided into two terms of fourteen and sixteen weeks, respectively."[5]

The total enrollment for the year, Lord was proud to report, was 274 students: 234 men and forty women, of whom twenty-nine were college graduates in search of additional business education credentials. Many were local, but some came from across the nation: Boston University, Harvard, Yale, Brown, Colby, Wellesley, Temple, Tufts, Bowdoin, Clark, Massachusetts Agricultural, Radcliffe, Smith, Lehigh, Western Reserve, and the University of Missouri.

According to Lord's report, the most popular course was Elementary Accounting (103 students enrolled), followed by Commercial Law, Commercial Composition and Business English, and Economics. The rest of the curriculum blended courses in business organization, advertising, salesmanship, news reporting and writing, second-year accounting, the economic and tariff history of the United States, the industrial history of Europe, and elementary Spanish. Lord also arranged a significant number of guest appearances by Boston businessmen who were, he explained, "able to give the students the advantage of their practical experience," once again reflecting his passionate belief in the importance of combining the "cultural" and "practical."

The launch was declared a success by *Bostonia*, the university's official magazine, which reported, "The opening exercises of this new department added an impressive and stirring chapter to the history of the University. . . . Promptly at seven o'clock on the opening night the classes assembled, with few preliminary words the instructors began the work of the year."[6]

As the trustees had envisioned, the enterprise ran a small deficit in the first year—which was successfully covered by Lord's bonds. By the second year, tuition revenues exceeded expenses. The guarantors had recouped their investment.

THE LEGITIMACY CHALLENGE: SHADY PRACTICES AND "MALEFACTORS OF GREAT WEALTH"

Before the College of Business Administration could become a permanent part of Boston University, Lord and his colleagues faced a new threat: the difficulty of overcoming the "legitimacy obstacle." Lord had to convince President Murlin and the trustees that a full-time program of business study, with commitments to full-time faculty and significant physical resources, would be both financially sustainable and conceptually sound. In short, the College of Business Administration had to have a mission consistent with the high purpose of a university.

Many supporters of collegiate education objected to the very notion of teaching business subjects in a university. Proprietary commerce colleges were scorned as unprofessional or worse, and some trustees and supporters wanted to prevent Boston University's good name, and its Metholdist heritage, from becoming associated with the world of shady, unsavory business practices. This was, after all, the Progressive Era, when "caveat emptor" ruled and reformers such as Theodore Roosevelt railed against "malefactors of great wealth."

THE PURPOSE OF BUSINESS . . . AND BUSINESS EDUCATION

"This conception of business, this acceptance of service as its basic motive, is of the greatest ethical importance. It is not too much to say that in recognition of service rather than money making as a main purpose, business won its first great ethical victory."

—Everett W. Lord, *The Fundamentals of Business Ethics*, 1926

Lord, who had earned both his bachelor's and master of arts degrees from BU, explained the purpose of the College of Business Administration as one of raising professional standards, of integrating the "cultural" with the "practical," all in the "service to society." The idea of serving society through business education would guide the school—and shape its professional identity—for decades to come.

Once launched, the college reached a strategic turning point when the university's trustees authorized expansion of the evening program to a new, full-time program (Day Division) of study in the College of Business Administration. The

Day Division allowed CBA to increase its enrollment and revenue, making it financially viable for the university. CBA's financial contribution to the university helped secure its future. It also committed the school to a model of business professionalism.

Approval of the Day Division allowed BU to join a select group of fellow pioneers in full-time, professional business education that included the Wharton School at the University of Pennsylvania (founded in 1881);[7] New York University and Dartmouth's Tuck School of Business (both founded in 1900); the School of Commerce and Administration at the

University of Chicago (1902); the business school at Northwestern University (1908); and the Graduate School of Business at Harvard, established in March 1908. Columbia Business School would be established in 1916.[8] In time, some focused entirely on graduate studies (e.g., Harvard and Columbia) while others including BU, Wharton, and NYU would offer both undergraduate and graduate programs.

Boston University's journey into management education had begun. There would be no turning back.

NOTES

1. *Culture Shock 1913*, Studio 360, December 28, 2012. Episode #1352, originally broadcast on December 28, 2012. www.Studio360.org/2012/dec/28.

2. Kathleen Kilgore, *Transformations* (Boston: Boston University, 1989).

3. Kilgore, *Transformations*, 99. According to the board minutes, a minimum of $7,500 had to be guaranteed through bonds. Later accounts placed the number at $10,000.

4. Ibid.

5. President's Annual Report, Vol. 39, 1913-14, 28-31.

6. *Bostonia*, Vol. XIV, No. 3 (October 1913), 110.

7. Joseph Wharton's pioneering vision for the School was to produce graduates who would become "pillars of the state, whether in private or in public life." (Source: "Wharton History," *Wharton University of Pennsylvania*, accessed June 14, 2013, www.wharton.upenn.edu/about/wharton-history.cfm.

8. Columbia Business School was established in 1916 by the trustees of Columbia University to "provide business training and professional preparation for undergraduate and graduate students." ("History," *Columbia Business School*, accessed June 14, 2013, www7.gsb.columbia.edu/about/history.) The school began with eleven full-time faculty and an inaugural class of sixty-one students, including eight women. It expanded rapidly after receiving an endowment from the president of Chase Manhattan Bank. By 1920, it had 420 students.

CHAPTER TWO
THE POET OF THE COUNTING ROOM[1]

A Remarkable Leader

Everett W. Lord would remain the dominant player in events surrounding the school's development for the next quarter century, although his journey to the deanship was an unconventional one, to say the least.

Everett W. Lord was born in Surry, Maine, and his family moved, first to Bucksport, then to Ellsworth, Maine, where young "Willie" began school. His formal schooling was interrupted by sea voyages on ships captained by his father, Samuel L. Lord. Everett Lord's philosophy of education—and his love of combining the "practical" and the "cultural"—can be traced to his own unusual educational background. Homeschooled on both land and at sea until he was in his teens, at age fourteen he became a cook on his father's schooner. (Cooking in turn became an interest he never relinquished; as dean, he rose at five thirty every morning to bake his own banana-flour bread.)[2]

Willie received only intermittent schooling while at sea, and it was not until he was eighteen that he began high school in Ellsworth, Maine, taking examinations to qualify after being tutored by the local minister's wife. Once admitted, however, he graduated within three years. The following year, he taught a Latin course to his former classmates, then was recruited as subprincipal, and finally became Ellsworth's first "superintendent" of schools. "They made me superintendent because they could get me for less money than anybody else would accept," Lord quipped. He earned $550 a year.[3]

In 1897, at age twenty-five, Lord moved on, entering BU. He graduated as a member of the Class of 1900, alongside eighty-four women and fourteen other men. Lord was a charismatic leader, an avid traveler, a lifelong devotee of the Spanish language, and a man who made an impression. Named "Class Statistician" at BU, he delivered a graduation speech calculating the total height and weight of his fellow class members. Part of his charm was his worldly experience—he had traveled to Cuba, Puerto Rico, and many of the Caribbean islands in the years preceding the Spanish-American War.

On January 5, 1901, he married Myrtle Ruth King of Wellsville, New York, and returned to work as a regional school superintendent in Bellows Falls, Vermont. Soon after, he received a letter from President Theodore Roosevelt inviting him to serve as assistant commissioner of education in Puerto Rico,[4] where he spent six years, 1902–8, developing the public school system. Lord then recruited a dozen BU graduates to teach in his new place of residence, helping establish what would eventually become the University of Puerto Rico.

By 1906, the peripatetic Lord had returned home, having earned his master of arts (AM) degree from BU Graduate School in both pedagogy and Spanish literature. He turned his efforts to the National Child Labor Committee (NCLC), an advocacy agency dedicated to protecting children from labor abuse. He was named New England secretary in 1908, and unlike his first superintendent job, this position paid well, about $3,500 a year, and involved extensive correspondence and communication with business and political leaders.

It also embroiled him in controversy. Lord, on behalf of the NCLC, argued against the presence of minors in the sardine fishing industry of his native Maine, where children as young as seven or eight commonly wielded eighteen-inch-long knives in cold, wet, slimy conditions for ten to twelve hours a day.[5] Accidents were common; results, gruesome. Despite local opposition, strict standards were enacted in Maine.

Lord, a passionate advocate for child labor laws, engaged in a sharp exchange of letters to the editor of the *New York Times*, in which Lord challenged the appearance of children onstage in theatrical shows. "An employment which results in physical or moral disaster for a vast majority of the young children who engage in it," wrote Lord, ever the pragmatist, "must offer in exchange something much more practical and tangible than the 'development of the

theatrical instinct' before it can be accepted as profitable. Experience has provided that for the average child there is no place more dangerous, and but few less advantageous than the professional stage."[6]

THE "MORE MEN MOVEMENT"

Everett Lord's involvement in the leadership of Boston University developed during the time he worked at the NCLC. It began when he and fellow BU graduates became determined to see more men enrolled at the university. Lord joined former classmates Leonard P. Ayres and Fred Lawton, along with other graduates who resented BU's being called a "girl's college." The men discovered that the 1910 graduating class at the College of Liberal Arts had *nine times* as many women as men. They agreed to create and support a "More Men Movement," studying the causes of BU's gender imbalance and then finding ways to attract more men. In Lord's own words:

> While studying conditions, I campaigned
> for men and succeeded in bringing a few
> to the College; but we had little to offer
> them except a standard classical course
> of study such as was given at every other

college in New England. There was nothing of "college life," no athletics, no particular prestige, no financial inducements. Why should a live boy choose Boston University in preference to any one of a dozen other colleges?[7]

So Lord and his colleagues raised $1,600 to underwrite a survey of prospective male students. Their answer to the question of what BU could offer to young men: education for positions in the business community.

Lord's strategy of launching a business program to attract more males proved successful—but not just with men. In CBA's first year (1913–14), a total of 274 students enrolled (234 men, 40 women); in the second year (1914–15), 425 arrived. That spring, T. Lawrence Davis became the first—and only—graduate of the college (Class of '15). A slight man with a mop of dark hair, Davis went on to have a long career in administration at Boston University, rising eventually to become dean of the College of Practical Arts.

By CBA's third year (1915–16), enrollment had reached 675, and twelve men and women followed Davis, receiving their bachelor of

T. Lawrence Davis, first graduate of College of Business Administration (1915)

business administration (BBA) degrees. The next academic year, 1916–17, total enrollment had grown to 1,438 students, and that June, fifty-one graduates (forty-eight men, three women) received their BBA degrees. An additional nine were awarded masters of business administration.

The college clearly had a future, and neither administrators nor trustees could deny it.

"What Is Good and Needful"

By the mid-1920s, Dean Lord's vision and values had coalesced into a coherent perspective on the emerging professionalization of business. An increasingly visible player in the national education field, Lord argued for the importance of business colleges in a 1938 *Christian Science Monitor* article, comprehensively titled, "Commerce in the Higher Brackets: Business Having Become Too Complex for Most Men and Women Without College Training, Boston University, Among Other Institutions, Provides the Needed Preparation."[8] Among "educators and business men of the late 1890s," Lord wrote,

> There seems to have been general agreement that a college graduate of that day was out of place in business, yet that nothing less than a college course could provide sufficient training for business. . . . Business had become too complex for men without college preparation, while the college-trained men were wholly unprepared for the field of business.

> At Boston University the purpose was to found a school of college grade and character . . . [and] a curriculum squarely based on the thesis that what is good and needful for earning a living is likely to be good for study.

> This college maintains the theory that in a capitalistic democracy our leaders and executives, and, indeed, all our voters, need an intelligent appreciation of capitalism in its relation to democracy and human welfare. We have refused to recognize a distinction between the cultural and the practical, but believe, rather, that every subject of study may be, and should be, at once cultural and practical.

Lord supported this view with ample evidence, arguing that business education was, at base, a true "service to society." He noted the success of BU graduates "as prospective experts," citing their success in finding employment, even during the years of 1932 and 1933 when unemployment was rising. By bringing into the classroom emerging theories of how environmental factors affected workers, Lord believed, business students could in turn introduce these important ideas directly into the workplace. The benefits even provided a patriotic slant: Foreign students were enrolling in high numbers in U.S. business colleges, Lord noted, and by becoming acquainted with "American business methods they have made the American methods almost the standard of the world."

One of Lord's most passionate arguments about business's "service to society" stressed the invigorating impact of competition, proving that he was ever the capitalist at heart. The "vitalizing effect" of schools of business on other schools, he pointed out, fostered competition with liberal arts, to the benefit of students. Schools of engineering were also adding business administration to their programs, while colleges and the commercial departments of high schools were absorbing graduates of university-based business programs as new faculty, thereby "raising the standard of elementary commercial instruction." Finally, Lord highlighted the unique role of the Bureau of Business Research, which the college sponsored to provide reliable economic data, especially about New England industry.[9]

Dean Everett Lord had been building both his own and CBA's reputations as the realities of World War I and its aftermath placed great strain on employment practices in the United States. During the Great War, millions of young men were called to the nation's service, and replacement workers were drawn from a

pool of less qualified men and women vitally in need of education. Training in business principles became more essential, and the government called upon universities such as BU to assist in the effort. Lord himself served in both arenas: during the war, he headed the Federal Employment Service in Boston, a position he maintained while also serving as dean of CBA.

Boston University was one of four hundred universities selected by the federal government to create a Student Training Army Corps (STAC), devoted to training the estimated 200,000 officers who would be needed for the war effort. Although the war ended in November 1918, before the program reached maturity, many of the STAC students who started at BU stayed on, including many at CBA. A large number of veterans used their bonus money to pay tuition for business courses.

After World War I, the demand for business education grew even further. Throughout the nation, schools added new programs, courses, and classes as the professionalization movement steamed on. Enrollment soared, and at Boston University, matriculation rocketed by more than 100 percent: In 1920–21, 1,364 students were enrolled in the day and 2,542 in the evening programs; in 1924–25, day enrollment reached 1,441 while evening and special program enrollment topped 5,970; by 1928–29, enrollment hit 1,419 day and 4,474 evening and special program students. But along with this success came a new challenge.

TURNING POINT #2:
BUILDING A PLACE CALLED 'HOME'

The growing appeal of the College of Business Administration to students proved a double-edged sword: demand for courses could not be matched by equivalent growth in available classrooms. In fact, from the start, the quest for suitable physical space had been a recurrent theme in the college's history.

The first classes offered in 1913 had a makeshift air, held as they were in CLA classrooms at 688 Boylston Avenue. But by 1916, when the Day Division began, even that arrangement was doomed since there remained no more space at CLA.

"A Building But No College; a College But No Building"

Once again, an unexpected benefactor materialized just in time, in the form of George F. Willett, a university trustee whose initial plan—and long-harbored hope—had been to start a college for the education of public officials. His goal: to build what he referred to as a "college for mayors."

Willett had also been a guarantor, through purchased bonds, of the new College of Business Administration. In service of his plan for a "college for mayors," he had leased the Walker Building, located at 525 Boylston Street on Copley Square, owned but recently vacated by the Massachusetts Institute of Technology. In the words of Eleanor Rust Collier, author of the 1959 history *Boston University, College of Business Administration, 1913-1958*, "Mr. Willett had a building but no college; Boston University had a College, but no building."[10]

College-less, as it were, and eager to put his new building to good use, Willett authorized its remodeling. Cost: $60,000, of which the trustees would reimburse Willett for $20,000. Mandated time frame: six short weeks. Goal: occupancy in time for the start of the new academic year.

525 Boylston Street.
CBA's first home

By the fall of 1916, "525" became the new home for the College of Business Administration, where it stayed for twenty-three years until 1939.

"That We Shall Raise a Nobler Race of Men"

In 1919, Boston University's trustees anticipated that the university would one day need to consolidate its schools on one campus, and they purchased acreage in Brookline for this purpose. But by the late 1920s, BU's buildings were still flung across the city, with the Law School, Medical School, and CLA scattered among different neighborhoods.

When BU's new president, Daniel Marsh, arrived in 1926, the university drew up plans to centralize its dispersed colleges. Development of the Charles River campus became one of Marsh's long-term priorities. Although the Great Depression would threaten to stall, or crush, his ambitions, fate and a bit of luck led him to the doorstep of the College of Business Administration.

The property at 525 Boylston Street that CBA used was still owned by MIT, which sold the building to the New England Mutual Life Insurance Company as the site for the firm's new headquarters. BU was given six months to vacate.

The school's leaders protested, and MIT relented, but only for a year's time. Now, though, at least President Marsh had a workable window. Long before twenty-first-century politicians would make the phrase famous, Marsh decided to "never waste a crisis." His strategy was to develop the new campus by starting with a home for the College of Business Administration.

Marsh had previously commissioned drawings for buildings on the new Charles River campus, but then, lacking funds, he refused to set a date for breaking ground. Eventually, critics would see the wisdom in his hesitation: by the end of Black Tuesday in October 1929, the stock market had crashed, the Roaring Twenties had ended, and the nation was headed into an economic depression.

M.I.T's decision to sell "525" forced the issue for the trustees. Both Dean Lord and President Marsh pressed to confront head-on the challenges left in the wake of Black Tuesday—

including stalled building plans, declining enrollment, and struggling students unable to pay tuition—by combining bluntness, practicality, and an eye toward the depression's end. Deals were negotiated with students, helping them make partial payments and continue their education. Lord, among these creative dealmakers, commissioned a string of studies throughout the 1930s, showing that employers paid a premium for college graduates. His point: investment in a college education would likely yield higher wages when the economy was restored to health. CBA's enrollment declined less than any other unit at BU.

685 Commonwealth Avenue (Charles Hayden Memorial, circa 1939)

Although the decline in tuition revenue led President Marsh and trustees to impose salary reductions on faculty and staff, most CBA faculty stayed. Marsh, who had become known as the "benevolent dictator," was blunt about the options available to those who complained about the cuts.

Economic problems were not their only obstacles, however. The Commonwealth of Massachusetts exercised its power of eminent domain to take from Boston University 130,000 square feet of property along the Charles River, plus riparian rights, to construct Storrow Drive. This severed the campus from the riverbank and eliminated forever the plan for a campus that faced the Charles River. One upside remained: compensation from the Commonwealth's Metropolitan District Commission (MDC) amounted to more than $300,000, invaluable capital for development. Finally, the university was ready to put in motion Marsh's plan for a new campus.

President Marsh worked with Dean Lord and

BU trustee Ernest Howes, a Boston leather merchant, to raise funds for their first project, a five-story limestone structure to house the College of Business Administration. Tapping both alumni and friends, they raised 50 percent of the estimated $1.175 million cost. Marsh then turned to the Charles Hayden Foundation, established by Charles Hayden for the purpose of educating young men and boys. (Their argument was that, as CBA was primarily attracting young men, it fell within the spirit, if not the exact letter, of Hayden's will.)[11]

Charles Hayden painting and inscription

"THAT WE SHALL REAR A NOBLER RACE OF MEN WHO WILL MAKE BETTER AND MORE ENLIGHTENED CITIZENS TO THE ULTIMATE BENEFIT OF MANKIND"

CHARLES HAYDEN

Everett W. Lord, circa 1939

When the foundation agreed to provide precisely the missing 50 percent, the full $1.175 million goal was achieved. Marsh, Lord, and their team of trustees agreed that CBA's new home should be named the Charles Hayden Memorial. At the ground breaking, President Marsh climbed into the cab of the steam shovel, worked the levers, and scooped the first shovelful of Back Bay earth: far below the layers of decayed salt marsh and peat, the builders would eventually find a suitable foundation.

On Tuesday, September 26, 1939, the Charles Hayden Memorial was dedicated as the first building erected on the Charles River campus. It was almost one hundred years to the day since the university's first classes were conducted, which had taken place in the Green Mountains of Newbury, Vermont. In the lobby of the new CBA building, visible from the large bronze front doors, hung an oil portrait of the late Charles Hayden, placed just above a plaque bearing these words from Hayden's bequest:

> *That we shall raise a nobler race of men*
> *Who will make better and more*
> *   enlightened citizens*
> *To the ultimate benefit of Mankind.*

CBA's new home and its benefactor's bequest both echoed the promise upon which the college had been founded more than two decades earlier: education in "service to society."

"To the Goal Which Heaven Has Sent"

That fall, a great celebration marked the opening of Boston University's new Charles Hayden Memorial. Speeches, ceremonies, luncheons, dinners, and entertainment followed the dedication. The bespectacled, sharp-nosed chemist James B. Conant, then president of Harvard, joined the events, as did the great banker Wallace B. Donham, then serving as the second dean of Harvard Business School.

Although Hitler's aggression in Europe was already well under way, the opening was a triumph for both Boston University and Dean Lord. He was no longer the young, energetic academic entrepreneur. By now, Lord had worked with two presidents, helped shape the university's entire new campus, and put the College of Business Administration on the map as a successful and innovative school of management education. "The history of the college of business administration," wrote BU's Bureau of Publicity (forerunner of today's Public Relations Office), "is the history of Dean Lord for the past quarter of a century. Whatever the college is today, he made it."[12]

Everett Lord enjoyed his few years in CBA's new home. The nautical symbols he favored, including the ship model on his desk, were

Boston University

College of Business Administration

OUR BUSINESS CREED

WE BELIEVE

IN **TRUTH**, THE ONLY FOUNDATION OF SUCCESS:

IN **SERVICE**, THE MOTIVE OF BUSINESS:

IN THE **GOLDEN RULE**, THE UNCHANGING STANDARD OF CONDUCT:

IN THE CONSCIOUSNESS OF **SERVICE PERFORMED** THE SUFFICIENT REWARD OF ENDEAVOR.

IN CASE OF LOSS, FINDER PLEASE RETURN TO BOSTON UNIVERSITY

Business Creed, circa 1930. Graduates received a small leather case containing a replica of their diploma and the business creed. Permission to use by family of Farnum Johnson Pollard.

reminders of his youth in Maine and trips on his father's ship. The seal on the floor of the Charles Hayden Memorial features a ship, heading "Down East," a reminder of many of Lord's boyhood voyages.

By the mid-spring evening of May 17, 1941, Everett W. Lord had turned seventy, the university's mandatory retirement age, and he was feted at a celebratory dinner covered by the *Boston Sunday Post* (May 18, 1941):[13]

Universitatis Bostoniensis

IN CIVITATE MASSACHUSETTENSI.

SENATUS ET CURATORES,

OMNIBUS AD QUOS HAE LITERAE PERVENERINT SALUTEM IN
DOMINO SEMPITERNAM.

Scitotis Nos **Farnum Johnson Pollard** civem huius Universitatis titulo gradusque Bachelor of Business Administration adornavisse atque condecoravisse, eique fruenda omnia dedisse iura, privilegia, honores, dignitates, et insignia quae hic aut uspiam gentium ad illum Gradum evectis concedi solent.

In cuius rei testimonium literis hisce publicum Universitatis sigillum et chirographa usitata apponenda curavimus.

Datum ex aedibus Universitatis a.d. XVI Kal. Julias Anno Salutis MDCCCCXXX Reipublicae Americanae CLIV

Everett W. Lord
Dean College Business
Administration

UNIVERSITAS BOSTONIENSIS.
CONDITA MDCCCLIX.

Daniel L. Marsh
Praeses.

Gaspar G. Bacon,
Scriba Curatorum.

In a programme [sic] starred with warm wishes, messages of appreciation, presentation of gifts, speeches and music, an alumni group of more than 600 graduates of the Boston University College of Business Administration gathered last night in the college's new home, the Charles Hayden Memorial, at 685 Commonwealth Avenue, and paid tribute to their first and only dean, Everett W. Lord, 70, who next month will

The dean received several gifts: President Daniel Marsh announced that the trustees had voted a pension for Dean Lord, "an unprecedented action," wrote the *Post* reporter, "inasmuch as the retirement pension plan recently adopted by the university does not go into effect until 1946 and Dean Lord would not have come under its provisions."

Among Lord's other gifts: a desk, two chairs, and the first-ever gold order awarded by Alpha Kappa Psi, the national professional honor society, "for the service which [Lord] has rendered to the fraternity in national research and in office, in personal work and in cooperative effort of meritorious nature for the advancement of the fraternity interests."

But the gift receiving the greatest applause, according to reports, was from the school's graduates. They presented Lord with a work order for a landscaper to completely finish the grounds of his new home in Falmouth Foreside, Maine,

"which will include a flagpole decorated with a brass plate suitably inscribed . . . indicating the gift presented . . . on behalf of the business college's alumni."

Lord's last recorded words as dean of the College of Business Administration were these:

Tonight as I look back over 70 happy years I am thankful . . . that so large a part of those years has been spent in the field of education. Yet . . . as I near the end of the road I sing no swan song. I pen no jeremiads. I am rich in your friendship. I am happy in your affection. With profound gratitude for all the blessings of the past and for what you, my friends, have shown of your feeling for me, my only word is now, "Go on and on, and to an ever more fruitful future," to higher attainment—to the goal which heaven has sent and which we reach with heaven's help.

Events would soon prove that the "fruitful future" Lord hoped for would not easily be achieved.

NOTES

1. Max R. Grossman (Class of '27), "Ye Olde Family Album: Dean Everett W. Lord," *Bostonia*, January 1932, 8-28ff. Everett Lord maintained contact with a wide and varied group of professional colleagues, students, faculty, and friends. He also enjoyed poetry and was given to rhymes in iambic pentameter. One popular poem was entitled "The Business of Business." Henry Ford was said to have a copy on his office wall. This talent was often mentioned by colleagues, leading to Lord's reputation as the "poet of the counting room."

2. Lord's affection for banana flour was tied to a health problem, possibly diabetes, because he was required to avoid the consumption of sugar. He also consumed raw vegetables and was reputed to have carried bags of fruit and vegetables to luncheon speaking engagements so he could avoid eating the plated meal.

3. Ibid.

4. This was his "dream job," but there is no explanation as to how President Roosevelt was persuaded to make the appointment.

5. Charles Scontras, *In the Name of Humanity: Maine's Crusade Against Child Labor* (Augusta: University of Maine Bureau of Labor Education, 2000).

6. Everett W. Lord, letter to the editor, *New York Times*, July 3, 1910. Lord mistakenly referred to "Mrs. Frances Moran" with the Reverend Francis Moran who actually wrote the original letter to the editor.

7. Collier, "College of Business Administration," 4.

8. Everett W. Lord, "Commerce in the Higher Brackets: Business Having Become Too Complex for Most Men and Women Without College Training, Boston University, Among Other Institutions, Provides the Needed Preparation," *Christian Science Monitor*, May 4, 1938.

9. Ibid.

10. Collier, "College of Business Administration," 5.

11. Kilgore, *Transformations*, 184.

12. "Impressive Dedication Program Planned at Boston University for Opening of New Charles Hayden Memorial Home of the College of Business Administration – Monday September 18, thru Saturday October 7, 1939," *Boston University Bureau of Publicity, Special Bulletin* No. 799 (Boston: September 24, 1939): 4.

13. "Dean Lord Given Unusual Tribute," *Boston Sunday Post*, May 18, 1941.

CHAPTER THREE
POSTWAR BUSINESS EDUCATION 1941-73

Business Education in Wartime America

Dean Lord's retirement preceded the U.S. entry into World War II by just a few months.

William Sutcliffe was named dean and given the responsibility of navigating CBA through the many crosscurrents of the 1940s and 1950s. The college suffered a significant enrollment decline during the early 1940s. The wars in Europe and the Pacific produced a national mobilization that hit traditional college life hard. In CBA, so many members were in uniform that the school had to suspend its popular "extern" program of a year's supervised employment. Men and women students also left in large numbers for high-paying defense plant jobs. The downsizing was necessary, as was the rationing of food, oil, and other necessities. As opportunities opened for women, however, the college offered programs to ease their entry into the workforce.

"I Am Professor of a Subject That No Longer Exists"

Bill Sutcliffe was an economist with a whimsical sense of humor. He named his Irish setter Dignity and his wirehaired fox terrier Impudence. Born in Chatham, Kent, in England, he had first attended a Wesleyan school for boys and considered a future career in government service. But at age thirteen, his family moved to British Columbia where his father became the superintendent of construction at a large lumber mill,

and Bill became an apprentice machinist. Although Sutcliffe would one day go on to become Dean Everett W. Lord's successor, leading CBA through World War II and its transformative aftermath, his early experience working at the mill anchored him in the real world of the workplace.

Sutcliffe attended the University of British Columbia in Vancouver, served in the ROTC, and then in 1919 won a scholarship in economics to attend Harvard. In 1920 he went to teach at Simmons College, publishing his first book, *Elementary Statistical Methods*, in 1925. By 1927, Sutcliffe had arrived at Boston University as an assistant professor, leaving for a year in 1931 for Hamline University in St. Paul, Minnesota, and then returning to BU as full professor of economics. Among his other roles: associate director of the Bureau of Business Research, educational director of the Boston Chapter of the American Institute of Banking, and director and then associate dean of the graduate division of the College of Business Administration.

Sutcliffe, a gifted speaker, conversed easily with audiences ranging from labor unions to banking officials. On the theme of business education, he admired Everett Lord greatly; English universities, less so. "He was a pioneer in his field," Sutcliffe said of his predecessor, "and since the founding of this school here, many institutions along similar lines have been established throughout the country." But across the pond, British universities "have not developed specialized business training . . . to anywhere near the same degree that we have here in the United States," Sutcliffe lamented. "Boys and girls here are lucky to have these opportunities; the great enrollment—nearly 3,500—must, of necessity, indicate the tremendous social service being rendered by the college here."

On June 15, 1941, just a few short weeks after Dean Lord's retirement party, the *Boston Sunday Post* profiled Sutcliffe, writing, "There is no carpet in the office of William G. Sutcliffe, newly appointed dean of the Boston University College of Business Administration, so nobody will be called up on it!"[1] Sutcliffe's own personality and humor, as well as his straightforward style, would shine through many of his own quips. Asked once by a reporter about modern economics, he responded, "I am professor of a subject that really no longer exists, since it is being

Dean William Sutcliffe

emasculated by the controversies that have arisen over the New Deal economics and those of the classical school. There is nothing tangible left in the world of economics to hang on to, but we still have to teach it."

"Guns and Butter"

When Sutcliffe was asked, "Just what are economics?" he answered, "The best and simplest definition is that economics is the science of business in its social aspects. But what's happened to business? There are a lot of social aspects but not much business." Looking ahead to the inevitable wartime economy, Sutcliffe predicted that the country could not have both "guns and butter"— and the future would call for less "butter" until Hitler could be defeated.

But Sutcliffe argued for the value of a business education, especially in such times: "There certainly is . . . [value] for a boy or girl to go to college in this war-torn world, especially to business colleges," he urged. "Government is suffering such a shortage of management they are actually under contract to Proctor & Gamble and the Goodyear Rubber Company . . . to supply managerial ability."

The dean closed this interview with a strikingly modern perspective. "One of the things I have learned in teaching is that students must be permitted at all times to express opinions of their own," Sutcliffe insisted, "and to defend them, even if they run counter to the teachings of the professor or the trends of the times."[2] He then offered a stirring defense of intellectual open-mindedness as the soul of the educational process, an observation that rings true today as the school moves into its second century.

DEATH, WAR, AND THE MODERN BUSINESS SCHOOL

World War II extracted a high price from Boston University and its students. The military draft diverted thousands of young men and women toward military service. Total enrollment at the university dwindled to 6,000 by the fall semester of 1943, of whom 60 percent were women. CBA enrollment dropped to 436 students in the Day Division. According to the university's records, 223 BU students and graduates were killed in the European and the Pacific wars.

The university's fortunes would take a favorable turn as quickly as they had fallen. In 1944, in response to FDR's State of the Union call for fresh thinking about the "postwar world," the university developed a program of conferences,

DEAN SUTCLIFFE'S EDUCATIONAL PHILOSOPHY

Freedom of discussion is the essence of education. We are dealing with a dynamic society, so teaching and learning must be dynamic, instantly ready for any new set of circumstances which may arise. The day of learning facts and theories by rote is definitely over.

—Dean William Sutcliffe

courses, and workshops focused on planning for a postwar era that would be dramatically different from the past.

At 7:00 p.m. on August 13, 1945, President Truman made a radio address to the nation and announced the surrender of Japan. In Boston, as elsewhere, a massive celebration took place. While mourning for the scores of BU graduates and former students who had died in the war, the university also recognized with pride the 1,132 who had been decorated with honors ranging from the Congressional Medal of Honor to the Purple Heart.[3]

Standing in front of the Boston University community on commencement day in the spring of 1946, General Dwight D. Eisenhower received his first American honorary degree. His reflections touched on the terrible recent losses of the war, and the general suddenly departed from his prepared text, asking, "Why doesn't Dr. Marsh and the president of every great university throughout the world teach his people to put people in my profession permanently out of business?"

Eisenhower's spontaneous wish may not have come true, but education boomed in the postwar era, forcing significant changes in college life. On a September morning in 1945, for example, more than 20,000 prospective students showed up to register for classes, breaking all previous attendance records. More than 6,000 were veterans, supported by the GI Bill of Rights. They led the wave of university enrollment, which by 1947–48 pushed total BU enrollment to 30,694, five times the wartime low.

NEW REALITIES, NEW COMPETITORS

The postwar enrollment bubble was exciting, but it also portended future problems. Student numbers outstripped on-campus housing facilities, forcing thousands of BU attendees into the city's neighborhoods and contributing to its "commuter school" image.

Business education was being transformed as well. The "new realities" produced some surprising innovations in the College of Business Administration. Many CBA students were married and lived off campus. For the first time, the school offered two unusual B-school courses called Marriage and Courtship Problems, led by a sociology professor who had taught at the University of Shanghai in China.[4] Social change was suddenly sweeping over CBA, just as it had begun to do with the conventions of larger society.

The enrollment bubble lasted until the 1950s but eventually fell victim to shifting demographics, a downturn in New England's manufacturing sector, and the rising popularity of new fields such as communications, science, and technology too.

Competition was growing from within BU. From one corner, it emerged in the figure of a communications entrepreneur named Howard LeSourd, who was determined to start a School of Public Relations on the Charles River campus. Although CBA had been offering a popular journalism program since classes started in 1913, had forged close relationships with Boston newspapers and other print media, and offered an extensive on-the-job training program, LeSourd's vision targeted one of the college's weak spots. New technology in radio, film, television, and sophisticated print media had begun to undermine CBA's traditional approach.

LeSourd opened his new initiative, BU's School of Public Relations (SPR), in September 1947. That first fall, enrollment reached 452 students, rising to 656 by the end of the academic year. The forerunner of the School of Public Relations and Communications (known today as the College of Communications) had been

launched. The following year, President Marsh announced that, in honor of the new SPR, 1948's Founders' Day would be devoted to an Institute on Public Relations, called "Social Responsibilities of American Leadership." Like a new market upstart, SPR gathered even more momentum when four faculty members from CBA's Journalism Department moved to the new school to establish its journalism division.

TUMULT AND TURNOVER

When Dean Sutcliffe retired in 1958, he could look back on seventeen years of leadership at CBA. Together with Everett W. Lord, the two deans had provided consistent, stable direction for the college for almost half a century. This stability would be significantly challenged over the next fifteen years.

The university chose Philip H. Ragan, a business consultant, as CBA's third dean. Little remains known about Dean Ragan's agenda, however, and he barely served four years (1958–62) before resigning. Professor James W. Kelley, chairman of the CBA Economics Department, stepped in after Ragan's departure, being named dean ad interim for the 1962–63 academic year. Kelley, a respected scholar

Dean John Fielden with baseball great Jackie Robinson at CBA "Men in Management" Event, 1967

and former chair of the Bureau of Business Research, provided a brief but crucial period of stability. Then, as his interim year of stewardship closed, new sources of turmoil—social, economic, and political—challenged the school.

John ("Jack") Fielden, an associate editor of the *Harvard Business Review*, was next to take the helm. Although Fielden presided as dean from 1963 to 1971, his time at BU proved turbulent, marred by student protests of the Vietnam War, the draft, and the university administration. At CBA, enrollments fell, leading to belt-tightening. Boston, as in many U.S. cities, faced civil unrest and street riots; meanwhile, the economy stumbled. The murders of President John F. Kennedy (1963), Robert Kennedy (1968), and BU alum Dr. Martin Luther King Jr. (1968) had left the nation in mourning and with a pervasive sense of unease. By 1971, Fielden had resigned, headed for Alabama to establish a business school at the University of Alabama–Birmingham.

Next, Arthur Thompson, an internationalist, author of a well-known textbook on business strategy and policy, and former head of BU's operations in Europe, stepped in to take Jack Fielden's place. Before two years passed, BU's financial problems felled him, too, sinking a string of Thompson's proposals. By 1973, he had resigned. The college had counted four deans in a decade and a half.

This turnover, which caused instability for CBA, occurred in the context of the larger university and national educational challenges that had been brewing since the early 1960s. Among the many agitations of the time in America, students were questioning the proposition that college education—much less *business*

education—was worth the effort and expense.

Business education in particular was being put under the social microscope. Starting in 1959, the Ford Foundation had issued an influential critique of business education. Informally known as the Gordon-Howell Report but officially titled *The Education of American Businessmen*, this document had launched a wave of new thinking that, for the next two decades, challenged deans, presidents, and trustees to rethink the very mission of the business school.

The Ford Foundation report criticized institutes of business education for their narrow, trade-focused curricula; for employing poorly trained faculty; for attracting academically inferior students; and for implementing simplistic teaching and research methodologies. The report's focus on the need for rising standards renewed emphasis on "the disciplines." Reminiscent of Everett Lord's focus on the "cultural" and the "practical," the Gordon-Howell authors emphasized the need to broadly educate future leaders: "The main goal of a business education should be the development of an individual with broad training in both the humanities and principles of business, capable of independent, imaginative and constructive thought," they wrote. A business education, the authors argued, should help a student:

- acquire a general knowledge of his [and her] chosen field;
- develop his [and her] capacity to reason;
- develop a sense of values;
- help him [and her] to communicate more effectively.

The Gordon-Howell report also placed a renewed emphasis on ethics, as had Lord's vision of business education as a "service to society." They argued, "A business education should . . . develop in a student an inquiring, analytical and searching mind and a code of ethics including honesty, integrity and an uncompromising respect for the rights of others."

The Gordon-Howell Report was a major catalyst for business education reform, and its sponsors invested heavily to support its major recommendations, spending nearly $15 million to spur change. But much more would be necessary to complete the job. And although by the 1960s, CBA's faculty had begun rethinking the vision of business education at BU, another decade, and a deeper crisis, would be required to truly spur a vital strategic transformation.

Growth, Ambition, and Clashing Visions: The Silber Era Begins

In 1971, Boston University trustees hired the institution's new president: John Silber, a forty-four-year-old philosopher and former dean of the College of Arts and Sciences at the University of Texas at Austin. Silber was well educated, an outstanding teacher, a tough debater, and "a man who put his beliefs into practice."[5] He was fired in July 1970 after the Regents voted to split his college into three parts, a move

President John Silber

Silber vigorously opposed. In coming to Boston University, Silber recognized both the dire financial straits facing BU and the need for academic and administrative reorganization. Conversant with the recommendations of the Gordon-Howell Report, Silber turned his focus to the College of Business Administration, in part because of its large enrollment and the cash surplus the business school was capable of generating, while many other units operated at a deficit.

President Silber commissioned McKinsey & Company to study the strategic future of BU. Peter P. Gabriel was the McKinsey partner in charge of the project. Gabriel had come to know Silber in Germany, and he so impressed the new president that Silber recruited him to be the business school's next dean. Gabriel's early efforts to revitalize the business school marked the beginning of the third strategic turning point in the evolution of the school.

In Gabriel's view, positioning Boston University for the competition of the 1970s required significant changes. He started with the school's name. In a sequence of internal memos, Gabriel argued for evolving the College of Business Administration to become a true School of Management.

TURNING POINT #3: UNVEILING SMG

On July 27, 1973, Gabriel circulated his ideas and solicited reactions from the faculty. At an August 28 faculty meeting, the discussion turned "spirited," but Gabriel made his vision clear: "We are a school of management and for management. As such, we are concerned with teaching, research and problem-solving related to all kinds of organized activity and to all kinds of institutional settings, private and public, in which such activity takes place."[6]

In a follow-up memo, Gabriel went further. In his trademark style, he argued that the objective was nothing less than "to become one of the country's foremost centers of education, research, and innovation in the functions and techniques of management of private and public institutions."[7]

All the other objectives, he argued next, should be governed by this objective.

Driving his point home, Gabriel urged the faculty to view this challenge through the lenses of both competition and necessity:

It implicitly rejects the alternative of our becoming (or continuing to be) a "good school," an "us-too" institution. . . . Any lesser aspiration would eventually force us to compete not on the basis of quality but on the basis of cost. Cost competition, in turn, would lead inexorably to a continuous lowering of quality and ultimately to our defeat by schools that are either heavily subsidized (like the University of Massachusetts), better endowed, or run below the minimum standards we would be willing to accept under any circumstances.

Gabriel's vision was shared by President Silber: private universities such as BU were significantly disadvantaged when competing with taxpayer-subsidized public universities. But this vision clashed—sometimes sharply—with some faculty, alumni, and supporters.

Dean Peter P. Gabriel

"Nothing More or Less Than the Recognition That We Have No Other Alternative"

Gabriel took on the argument of some self-described "realists," who argued that BU had to lower its sights. He insisted, "Thus, far from being a brave, heroic, or pie-in-the-sky flight of fancy, the objective of becoming one of the best, of aiming not at 'high' but *the highest* standards of quality and performance is nothing more nor less than reasoned recognition that we have no other alternative."

Then Gabriel leveled a challenge directly at CBA's faculty. If the school were to succeed, he argued, everyone had to be on board, together:

Whether an affirmation of free choice or a recognition of the indispensible, the proposed objectives collectively are no doubt the most ambitious CBA has ever contemplated. . . . To be sure, working toward their achievement will stretch all of us to the limit. They will require the greatest of ingenuity in the conception of strategies and plans, the greatest of resolve in the making of difficult decisions and trade-off choices, the greatest of determination and single-mindedness in carrying them out. They will challenge the best we have to give as individuals and as a group. There will be no room at the School for "let-George-do-it" attitudes. Nor shall we be able to afford the luxury of "every man for himself."

The discussion extended for months. Finally, in March 1974, Gabriel formally requested that the Executive Office and board of trustees approve that "that the name of the College of Business Administration (CBA) be changed to School of Management (SOM)":

We believe the former [title] no longer connotes faithfully the content of our current programs, much less that of the teaching and research activities we plan for the future. . . . Our intended focus not only on management in business contexts but also on management in its rapidly growing institutional settings outside the conventional business sectors should be reflected in our name.

Moreover, Gabriel, noted, a "college . . . tends to be more commonly associated with undergraduate education alone," obscuring the school's growing master's program and plans for a future doctoral program, targeted to launch by 1976.

Finally, Gabriel noted the objections, "mainly emotional as they may be," from alumni: "We are confident that most of this opposition will change to wholehearted support once the full rationale of our proposal is made known," the dean assured the school's graduates. "Whatever the residual opposition may be, we do not feel that the counterarguments can come even close to offsetting the real and significant benefits of the proposed name change." The trustees approved the proposal, and within a few months, the school's new direction would be reflected in the growing size and caliber of its faculty, including a dozen new members recruited from universities across the nation, from Iowa and Michigan State to MIT and Harvard to UC Berkeley.

"CBA Is Dead—Long Live SMG"

The bruising battle over names finally ended on July 18, 1974, when Dean Gabriel sent a memo to all senior officials in the university, as well as faculty and staff, titled "CBA Is Dead—Long Live SMG." As of August 1, 1974, the designation "College of Business Administration" ceased to exist at BU, replaced by the "School of Management." "Under our new name," Gabriel wrote, "as a school of management and for management in the broadest sense of

this function, we are committed to building SMG into one of the foremost centers of management teaching and research in the country—and to honoring thereby the sixty-year-old tradition associated with the CBA name we are about to retire."

A new era had begun.

NOTES

1. Leo Rabbette, "Dean Sutcliffe of BU, Noted Economist, Says His Subject is Puzzling, Even to Experts," *Boston Sunday Post*, June 15, 1941, A-1.

2. Ibid.

3. Kilgore, *Transformations*, 209.

4. Ibid., 212.

5. Kilgore, *Transformations*, 322.

6. Peter P. Gabriel, memorandum to CBA Faculty, "The Boston University School of Management," September 5, 1973.

7. The second objective is "to serve as a focal point of management education for the various professional disciplines represented by Boston University's schools and colleges." The third objective is "to contribute through problem-solving and direct service activities, along the entire range of the School's capabilities and competencies, to the life and welfare of the City of Boston, the New England region, and society at large." (Peter P. Gabriel, memorandum to faculty, September 11, 1973.)

CHAPTER FOUR
THE MODERN ERA 1974-2010

Governance Crisis

Peter Gabriel's vision of a professional school of management outlasted its creator.

45

As the new School of Management began operations, its progress was threatened by the larger politics of the university. In 1976, John Silber had been president for five turbulent years, a time defined by repeated clashes with faculty over salaries, budgets, faculty appointments, and unionization. That April, during one of the most famous and vitriolic conflicts in university history, Silber drew a faculty vote of "no confidence."

At a special meeting of the trustees, ten of the fifteen deans of BU's schools and colleges, including Peter Gabriel, called for President Silber's resignation. Silber, showing his trademark fighting spirit, refused, igniting a monthlong battle for leadership. The university's Board of Trustees had a decision to make. On April 27, after hours of meetings, a majority voted to back Silber. Gabriel resigned as dean a few days later.[1] Asked how one moves on after a fracas of such proportions, Silber, according to the *Boston Globe*, responded, "You do the same thing you do when you have a quarrel with your wife. You kiss and make up. I will refrain from kissing the deans."[2]

Despite his abrupt departure, by the time Peter Gabriel resigned in May 1976, he had changed the School of Management in three important ways. First, the school had been renamed and its mission reinterpreted. Second, important programs had been launched—including the master's concentration in health-care management, the master's concentration in public management, and a doctor of business administration program—that would help differentiate the school from its competitors and raise its academic profile. Third, Gabriel had recruited dozens of new faculty, whose scholarship and teaching would influence the direction of SMG for decades.

AFTER THE STORM: NEW GROWTH

Personality and policy clashes aside, Gabriel, Silber, and the faculty had all shared one thing: a vision of excellence, which flourished despite the turbulence. The 1980s would prove a period of innovation and growth at SMG. By the end of the 1980s, SMG enrollment reached around 3,500 undergraduate and graduate students per year, confirming its status as the second largest school in the university. The faculty had also grown in number, from the low thirties in the early 1970s to more than one hundred by the end of the 1980s. These newcomers infused new energy into the school, establishing research institutes, innovative programs, and ties with industry and government.

Once again, along with the school's growth, inadequate classroom and administrative space proved a problem. The building at 685 Commonwealth Avenue could no longer accommodate necessary classrooms, new computer labs, faculty offices, meeting space for recruiters, and offices for student counseling, so the school's facilities became dispersed. Most faculty offices were relocated to nearby brownstone buildings at 212 and 226 Bay State Road, or across Commonwealth Avenue (convenient, many faculty were pleased to note, to Mel's Diner); later, whole departments moved to 621 Commonwealth Avenue, space once occupied by the Lahey Medical Clinic near Sherborn Street (now named Silber Way).

Although its operations were geographically scattered, SMG thrived. By 1987, an Executive MBA (EMBA) program had been created, with classes offered in suburban Tyngsborough, Massachusetts, at the former Wang Institute (named for entrepreneur Dr. An Wang, founder of Wang Laboratories, who donated the property to BU). At the same time, the school increased its nondegree executive education offerings. Then in 1989, an Accounting MBA program (AMBA) was established for liberal arts graduates who sought careers in accounting, with many of its students being supported by leading accounting firms. The school also introduced its Asian Management Program.

THE RISE OF SMG'S RESEARCH CENTERS—THE 1980S

One of the most important developments during the 1980s was the expansion of faculty research, a dimension on which many academic institutions evaluate their peers. Beginning in the early 1980s, SMG created a number of new research centers. Faced with the challenge of launching a series of entirely new institutes across various fields, the faculty created at least three different models, each with a distinct funding source and business constituency.

Human Resources Policy Institute

In 1981, Professor Fred K. Foulkes led the development of the Human Resources Policy

HRPI director, Professor Fred K. Foulkes (left), and SMG Dean Ken Freeman (right) congratulate former senior vice president, human resources, IBM, J. Randall MacDonald, recipient of the W. E. Burdick Award for service to the profession, October 19, 2012.

Institute (HRPI) as a partnership between SMG and top-level human resources executives from numerous global companies. Foulkes came to BU from Harvard, where he had been a young professor teaching personnel policy and human resources management. At BU, Foulkes helped create a new model of business-academic collaboration. He recruited a group of human resource executives from a dozen companies to become founding members of the Human Resources Policy Institute. Thirty years later, this membership organization consists of fifty global companies and is one of the premier research-based institutes in the human resources field. HRPI integrates multiple disciplines around human resource policy and has developed extensive linkages between the business community and the School of Management. The basic organizing mechanism is HRPI's semiannual meeting, during which members participate in sessions on leading-edge human resources topics and in roundtable discussions. The institute sponsors faculty and doctoral research, develops case studies, conducts executive development programs, and is an information resource for members.

Manufacturing Roundtable

The Manufacturing Roundtable's (MRT) founder, Professor Jeffrey Miller, came to BU in 1981 to teach in the field of operations management. Previously an executive at Dow Chemical, Miller had taught operations management at Harvard Business School and recognized the importance of America's manufacturing crisis. At BU, his new institute's goal was to bring together representatives from manufacturers to focus on the critical issues challenging the manufacturing sector during what *Business Week* called "the reindustrialization of America."[3] The roundtable's success with American companies led to a subsequent Global Manufacturing Roundtable that also included Japanese and European members. Together with faculty colleagues Tom Vollman, Robert Leone, Stephen Rosenthal, Jay Kim, and Janice Klein, Miller surveyed manufacturing practices, improvements, and total quality management innovations, continuing the roundtable's research into the 1990s.

DEVELOPMENT OF NEW DEGREES AND JOINT DEGREE PROGRAMS, 1971–1983

1971   Master of Engineering in Manufacturing and Master of Business Administration

1973   Master of Business Administration in Health Care Management

1975   Master of Business Administration in Public Management

1976   Doctor of Business Administration (DBA)

1981   Combined Juris Doctor and Master of Business Administration in Law and Health Care Management

1982   Joint Master of Business Administration and Juris Doctor

1983   Master of Science in Management Information Systems

1983   Joint Bachelor of Arts and Master of Business Administration

1983   Joint Master of Business Administration and Master of Science in Broadcast Administration

Public Affairs Research Group

Funded by foundation research grants, the Public Affairs Research Group was founded in 1981 to study the formation of a new phenomenon: the corporate public affairs function. Hundreds of companies were expanding their Washington presence and a group of BU faculty—James E. Post, Edwin A. Murray Jr., Robert B. Dickie, and doctoral students John F. Mahon, Patti Andrews, and Jennifer Griffin—were among the first business school experts to analyze Washington offices, political action committees, new forms of lobbying, and corporate citizenship programs. The research program continued into the mid-1990s, and evolved into a partnership with the National Wildlife Federation and the Corporate Conservation Council, an industry group, to develop the first environmental management curriculum taught in an American business school, an initiative that drew the attention of *Business Week* and the *Wall Street Journal*.[4]

These models helped inspire other centers, institutes, and programs, including the Entrepreneurial Management Institute (EMI); the Small Business Development Program; the Systems Research Center (developed by Professors Michael Lawson, John Henderson,

Lee Sproull, and N. Venkatraman); the Executive Development Roundtable (EDRT), founded by Douglas Ready and led by Douglas T. "Tim" Hall; and the Leadership Institute (led by Professor Lloyd Baird).

These research centers combined corporate membership, funding for cutting-edge research, and media attention. The commitment to research partnerships with leading businesses, and a focus on questions of importance to both academic and the business communities made Boston University School of Management a national leader in practice-oriented research. Both the business press and the university's leadership paid attention.[5] *Business Week* cited SMG for its "relevant research" in a 1990 article and this growing reputation was a point of pride, as noted in one of President Silber's reports.

The school also pioneered a host of new courses, degrees, and joint degree programs during this era, bringing the knowledge acquired from research to students through creative course and program design.

The Leaders Behind the Changes

This period of innovation and entrepreneurship took place during an era of fast-changing leadership at SMG. After Peter Gabriel's departure, associate dean **David Furer** (1976–77) was appointed dean, ad interim. Like Gabriel, Furer was an alumnus of Harvard Business School and McKinsey & Company. He was known for his low-key, analytic style that, after the turbulence of Gabriel's departure, bred confidence and generated relief among faculty, staff, and central administration officials. Furer was also known for his unpretentious humor: on the inside panel of his office entryway, visible only behind closed doors, hung a poster of a cat clinging to a tight wire. "Hang in there baby!" the poster urged.

By the next year, **Dr. Jules J. Schwartz**, formerly of Wharton, had been named dean. Schwartz was energetic, relished a challenge, and had a reputation as a gifted teacher. But he too clashed over budgets and leadership style with both President Silber and the SMG faculty. He resigned the deanship in 1979, turning his attention to teaching a course at SMG on business strategy and policy that proved highly popular with students, and, in 1985, earning

Dean Henry M. Morgan, circa 1985

the Metcalf Prize, the university's highest recognition of teaching excellence.

Henry M. Morgan (1979–86) was quickly named dean. Born in Honolulu, Morgan was educated in Hawaii, Connecticut, and Cambridge, Massachusetts, where he earned a PhD in chemistry from MIT. Morgan was a World War II veteran; former president of KLH Research and Development Corporation, a technology firm in Cambridge, Massachusetts; and former director of human resources at Polaroid, where he established one of the first diversity training programs in corporate America. In 1974, he joined the BU faculty after teaching briefly at Harvard Business School, serving as chairman of SMG's new Management Policy[6] department before assuming the deanship.

As SMG's leader, Henry Morgan focused on initiatives to expand research and advance the school's interests in the community. Long before the term became popular, he demonstrated "social entrepreneurship" as an investor, entrepreneur, and progressive thinker, particularly as a pioneer in the community banking movement of the 1970s, when he served as a director of the ShoreBank Corporation in Chicago. ShoreBank was unique in that it focused its lending on initiatives in the inner city and impoverished communities in Chicago, Cleveland, Detroit, and rural Arkansas, providing loans mostly to the small business entrepreneurs who lived in these communities.

Professor John Russell, Associate Dean

Morgan and his wife, Gwen—herself a pioneering scholar-practitioner in creating on-site day care programs—invested their time, talent, and resources in a variety of educational causes, including several BU ventures.

Morgan was viewed with affection by those who worked with him in this era. Jeffrey Miller, in an interview for this book, lauded Morgan's "humanity" and the grace he brought to the job. At a retirement dinner held in his honor, Morgan was cited by President Silber for his many accomplishments and integrity: "I think that the success of the past seven years at our School of Management has been the result of the intelligence, imagination, dedication and selflessness of Dean Henry Morgan."[7] Morgan and his wife used the occasion to make a $500,000 gift to the university to support SMG's study of entrepreneurship.

One of Dean Morgan's most consequential management decisions was the selection of Professor John R. Russell as his associate dean to succeed Michael Lawson. Russell had been a management consultant and professor of operations management at Harvard Business School before joining BU to help establish the school's Public Management Program; he later chaired the Management Policy department. Now, he was tasked with assuming responsibility for SMG's budget, operations, staffing, and internal activities, becoming the "inside" member of the School's "Mr. Outside, Mr. Inside" team.

Historically, SMG had long played an important role in the entire university budget, serving as a surplus generator: it boasted a large student body and an operating budget built on salaries rather than expensive technology or laboratories, like many of the university's other schools. Now Russell carefully managed the school's operations and budget, funding new opportunities while exercising close administrative control over salary costs.

Dean Morgan's experience as an executive and investor, coupled with John Russell's mastery of detail, served the school well in its budget negotiations, which could sometimes be contentious. This enabled the school's agenda for growth and development to be advanced during Morgan's seven years as dean. When both Morgan and Russell stepped down in 1986, the SMG community could look back on one of the most effective and respected leadership teams in its history.

George W. McGurn succeeded Morgan as dean. McGurn, a "specialist in financial management systems and productivity improvement in the public sector," according to a BU press release, had originally come to BU as director of the Public Management Program. He broadened its focus to include both the nonprofit and the public sector, and became a liaison between SMG and the BU team administering the school system in Chelsea, a city just north of Boston. The Chelsea project, to which Dr. Silber was deeply committed, involved a massive undertaking by BU to demonstrate that a primary and secondary school system in a low-income community could be turned around with improved administrative management, progressive classroom techniques, and well-trained, effective teachers. This initiative was a university-wide commitment: the School of Education took responsibility for teacher development, while SMG oversaw improving the administrative functions.

Dean McGurn also nurtured the school's international relationships, especially in Japan, where SMG developed a partnership with Sanyo Corporation and several other major corporations. On campus, the dean also began planning and fund-raising for a new School of Management building, to be located at 595 Commonwealth Avenue. His plans were ambitious and necessary, but they also contributed

to a budget deficit. Then in February 1991, after a series of years during which McGurn had been unable to reverse this budgetary shortfall, he resigned. Associate Dean Douglas T. ("Tim") Hall was named acting dean.

Enter Dean Lataif

The university launched an international search for a leader who could bring SMG's new building to fruition. In June, the university announced that Louis E. Lataif, a senior executive of the Ford Motor Company and a 1961 graduate of CBA would become dean of the Boston University School of Management. Dean Lataif was familiar with both the school and President Silber; he had received an honorary degree from Boston University while serving as president of the Ford Motor Company's European operations and had recently been featured in SMG's magazine, *The Manager* (May 1991).

Lataif had spent his adult lifetime thinking about business problems and the challenges facing the professional manager. He was a fountain of ideas about what needed to be fixed and how to do so. Few anticipated the scope and depth of the new dean's desire to lead SMG in bold new directions. Years later, when Lataif retired

Louis E. Lataif (SMG '61, HON '90) Allen Questrom Professor and Dean, 1991-2010

from BU in 2010, Professor Fred Foulkes made this observation in a letter celebrating Lataif's tenure:

Even though I was on the search committee that selected you, my colleagues and I did not necessarily expect that a businessman recruited as a business school dean would have a big impact on a school's curriculum. Businessmen deans are supposed to raise money, give speeches to alumni, students and parents and make sure that the institution is run in a business-like fashion. In your case, you were recruited to raise money to build a building, a new home for SMG, something your predecessors had been unable to do. Curricular innovation is supposed to come from the faculty.

But from the start, it was clear that you would be different. You not only had a vision (and a passion) for business education but also specific ways to make your vision concrete for both faculty and students.[8]

Upon his arrival, however, the SMG community fixed their hopes on a successful campaign to build a new home for SMG. Few, if any, foresaw the transformation that was coming. And few could have anticipated that Dean Lataif would serve for nineteen years in this position: second in length of service only to that of Everett W. Lord, with an impact that ranked alongside that of the founding dean.

Turning Point #4: The Move to 595 Commonwealth Avenue

SMG labored under a severe physical space handicap throughout the 1980s. The classroom facilities at 685 Commonwealth Avenue were outdated and unable to accommodate burgeoning undergraduate and graduate program needs. Faculty offices were located in scattered buildings and were also inadequate. Fortunately, the double-digit interest rates of the early 1980s were falling, stirring hope among the faculty and staff that debt financing of a new building was becoming feasible.

The university had been acquiring property close to the campus in the hope of one day creating a unified Charles River campus. During the 1980s, a few sites—notably the Peter Fuller Cadillac Building located at the intersection of Commonwealth Avenue and the BU Bridge—had been evaluated, but judged inadequate.

A breakthrough finally occurred in 1985, when David Karney, an alumnus and former university trustee, donated $500,000 to underwrite the initial architectural drawings for a new management building. Another breakthrough took place in 1990, when, on the occasion of his son Bahaa's graduation, Rafik B. Hariri, prime minister of Lebanon, donated a $10 million naming gift for the building to be located at 595 Commonwealth Avenue.

The university commissioned Cannon Design to design SMG's new home. It was an exciting design, complete with a six-story atrium, tiered classrooms, state-of-the-art technology in classrooms and computer labs, and attractive offices, meeting rooms, and gathering space.

Within a year, by 1992, a New Building Campaign Executive Committee and an International Campaign Committee were formed. Dean Lataif set to work courting prospective donors. Known as a consummate communicator, Lataif spoke eloquently, passionately, and endlessly about both the school's needs and its potential for greatness. His vision for the new SMG went beyond bricks and mortar, to a new way of thinking and doing management. This vision had begun to incubate many years earlier in his career at Ford, when he worked with W. Edwards Deming, a founder

of the pioneering Total Quality Management (TQM) movement. As dean, Lataif began to incorporate a new sense of the school's mission into his messages: "management not as it has been, but as it must be."

By early 1994, Lataif's efforts had begun to pay off: total phase one campaign commitments had reached $23 million. On May 21, 1994, dignitaries broke ground for the new building at 595 Commonwealth Avenue, signaling phase two of the $80 million Capital Campaign. The milestone event was capped by a black-tie "celebration banquet" in the Grand Ballroom at the Boston Marriott Hotel at Copley Place. This event was timed to commemorate both the school's eightieth anniversary of its founding and the ground breaking of its next home. As one attendee later wrote, the new building was a "statement to the world that BU was serious about business."[9]

The success of the building campaign was attributable to the many alumni and friends who contributed to the creation of the Rafik B. Hariri Building; they are recognized on a "wall of honor" in the lobby and on plaques

Groundbreaking, May 1994, Dean Lataif, left; Chancellor Silber, second from right

"Open for Business"—Rafik B. Hariri Building, circa 1996

throughout the building. Each one involves a story of commitment to SMG and a personal relationship with Dean Lataif.

As the 1990s came to a close, the School of Management was poised to capitalize on the advantages of its new facilities. Few could anticipate how turbulent the next decade would be.

NOTES

1. According to Kilgore, "Faculty votes of no confidence in college administrators were becoming commonplace at a time of declining income, budget cuts, and faculty unionization" (Kilgore, *Transformations*, 357). On April 2, 1976, the Faculty Senate Council passed a resolution citing a "lack of confidence in the policies and practices of the central administration with respect to budgetary and educational matters" (Kilgore, *Transformations*, 351). Shortly after this "limited no-confidence vote," ten of the fifteen deans called for Silber's resignation at a meeting

with trustees. He refused and the battle continued for another month. In the end, the trustees gave Silber a vote of confidence; a number of the deans left in short order. Silber reiterated a comment first made after the Faculty Senate Council vote: "You do the same thing you do when you have a quarrel with your wife. You kiss and make up. I will refrain from kissing the deans" (Kilgore, *Transformations*, 354; *Boston Globe*, April 28, 1976, 5).

2. *Boston Globe*, April 28, 1976, 5.

3. "The Reindustrialization of America," *Business Week Special Issue*, June 30, 1980. The Manufacturing Roundtable's decade of research culminated in the publication of Janice A. Klein & Jeffrey G. Miller, eds. *The American Edge: Leveraging Manufacturing's Hidden Assets* (New York: McGraw-Hill, 1993).

4. "And business schools have noted the change. Last fall, Boston University became the first to offer a course in environmental management, developed with corporations and an environmental group." (Quoted in "The Greening of Corporate America," *Business Week*, April 23, 1990, 98.); "Business Schools Take Account of Environment," *Wall Street Journal*, May 3, 1991, B1.

5. According to *Boston University, 1971–1986* (Boston: Boston University, 1986), 51–52, a report prepared on the occasion of John Silber's fifteenth anniversary as president, SMG had established seven "research constellations": "Support from and association with local and regional businesses has been augmented substantially through the establishment of seven research constellations (in human resources, information systems, entrepreneurial management, manufacturing, direct marketing, and management practices in Asia" and established a program of executive education courses.

6. The Management Policy Department was renamed Strategy & Policy Department and, subsequently, Strategy & Innovation Department. The department has included faculty specializing in strategic management, international management, and entrepreneurship.

7. "Boston University Salutes Outgoing Management Dean, Announces Major Gift," Boston University press release, September 15, 1986. Morgan's humility was remembered at a 2001 memorial service in his honor held in his hometown of Lincoln, Massachusetts. At the conclusion of the service, the overflow congregation sang a hymn he had requested which, in the words of one attendee, captured the essence of the man: "How Can I Keep From Singing?"

8. Fred K. Foulkes to Louis E. Lataif, May 13, 2010, in *Transformational Leadership: A Celebration of Louis E. Lataif*, 21.

9. John DiCocco to Louis E. Lataif, May 13, 2010, in *Transformational Leadership: A Celebration of Louis E. Lataif*, 17.

CHAPTER FIVE
A NEW MILLENNIUM

Trying Times

The new building created a sense of optimism in the **SMG** community as the twentieth century closed.

This optimism would soon be tested in an era of social, technological, and political turmoil: from experts' fears over the tech impact of Y2K; to the health-care challenges of AIDS, SARS, and swine flu; to the contested 2000 presidential election; to the dot-com bubble, and the dramatic effects of 9/11.

9/11

The 9/11 attack on the World Trade Center in 2001 killed more than 3,000 people, including thirty-four BU graduates.[1] The catastrophe also had a direct effect on much of the Boston University community. The families of many BU students lived and worked in the New York,

September 11, 2001

New Jersey, and Connecticut metropolitan area, raising concerns about the safety of loved ones. In the early hours of the 9/11 crisis, BU officials closed the high-rise dormitories on campus, fearing possible attack. "We had to act" immediately, recalls Assistant Dean Sandra Procopio, since "no one knew the real risk at that time."

SMG students were encouraged to stay at 595 Commonwealth Avenue while officials assessed the campus security and staff members from the Undergraduate Program Office organized the delivery of sandwiches, cookies, and drinks. In the weeks that followed, especially given Boston University's large international student population, campus life remained in flux. Some of the university's foreign students decided to leave once travel became possible again, but most stayed.

MARKET COLLAPSE

Between March 2000 and October 2002, the U.S. stock market lost $5 trillion in value. The collapse severely impacted the job market for graduates, and starting salaries dropped sharply: in 2001, the average starting salary of MBA graduates had been $97,705, but it plunged to $87,005 in 2002 and $70,355 in 2003 (finally beginning its recovery in 2004, rising 11 percent to $78,299).[2]

The imploding market affected enrollments throughout Boston University. At SMG, freshman enrollments ranged from 406 in 2002 to a low of 315 in 2003, then to 375 in 2004.[3] Graduate enrollments were also volatile. The school's MS•MBA and Executive MBA (EMBA) Programs—whose students were supported by employers—suffered in particular, as companies cut spending. Enrollment declines posed a real threat to BU, since the university depended on tuition revenue, and its endowment fund, now sharply reduced in size due to the market decline, could not cover shortfalls.

But SMG maintained a clear strategic vision. In the 2001–2 annual report to the president, Dean Lataif described four areas of strategic focus: innovating new and improving existing curricula; building faculty excellence; creating an enhanced student experience; and promoting the work of the school. For each area, Lataif included a specific list of individual priorities for action.

The holistic nature of his strategic focus for SMG reflected Lataif's long-standing passion "to accomplish what other business schools have failed to do over the decades, namely to produce builders and leaders who are trained to think systemically (horizontally)."[4] With this vision, Lataif argued, Boston University School of Management could help build its "ideal" graduates, those who

are keenly sensitive to the interdependence of business decisions and to the effect of unintended consequences of decisions. They understand well the implications of management systems (what's measured and what's rewarded) on individual and collective behavior. They understand how to create, participate, and lead effective teams. They intuitively think cross-functionally about problems and solutions. Moreover, their perspective is genuinely global.[5]

Putting this vision into action, the faculty made *cross-functional thinking* a hallmark of the curriculum in both the undergraduate and MBA programs. Courses themselves became linked to one another in new and creative ways, demolishing the old departmental "silos." Innovations such as the freshman course Management as a System and junior year Core course, which integrated multiple areas of functional expertise, became SMG's unifying and defining experiences for undergraduates.

Another emphasis was *team learning*—a concept, Lataif stressed, distinctly different from group work. At SMG, students would learn the process of forming teams, contracting among team members, negotiating work assignments, and creating the magical synergy of genuine collaboration. The faculty itself worked in teaching teams as they integrated team learning into their courses and programs. Impressed by the importance of this model for future workers, managers, and leaders, the General Electric Foundation funded the school's Center for Team Learning.

BUILDING A NEW TEAM

The opening of "595" gave rise to important changes in the school's administrative leadership. The complexity of the school's programs and operations and the departure of a number of the senior administrators led to a reconfiguration of responsibilities. Senior Associate Dean Edwin A. ("Ted") Murray Jr. returned to teaching, as did Professor Jeffrey Miller, who had served as associate dean for academic programs. Assistant Dean for Finance and Administration Stephen Hannabury was recruited to become vice president of the new Olin College of Engineering. Dean Lataif

Teams at work in the
new building

reached into the faculty to rebuild the school's leadership team. John Chalykoff, chairman of the Information Systems Department, was named to succeed Miller, and Michael Lawson was named associate dean (and then senior associate dean) for the second time, having previously served in that role in 1977–81, with responsibility for faculty recruiting and development. Lawson would serve in this new role for another decade. Martin (Marty) Carter became assistant dean for finance and administration, and Professors Janelle Heinecke and Bill Bigoness also served in the new administration.

RECOGNIZING IT'S GROWING ROLE IN "MANAGEMENT AS A SYSTEM"

Recognizing that information systems were becoming indispensable in every functional area of the organization, and that few businesses or nonprofits had sufficient talent to strategically manage IT's growing importance, the school created one of its signal innovations: the MS•MBA degree. This new program enabled a student to earn both a master's in information systems and an MBA, and included an intensive field internship at one of SMG's corporate partners. Scholarship support helped the school attract highly qualified applicants, and sixty-seven MS•MBA students graduated in the first class,

Starbucks provided a welcome social and work setting

many having completed both a summer and a field internship during their course of study.

The importance of information technology across management led the school not just to create its new MS•MBA, but also to refine its entire research and teaching mission. It adopted an original tagline, "fusing the art, science, and technology of business," to document IT's new, central role in its existing goals of teaching "management as a system" and team learning. "By *fusing the art, science, and technology of business in our teaching*," the 2006–7 annual report claimed, "we impart knowledge of business disciplines with a unique cross-functional perspective to prepare ethical, innovative leaders for the good of society worldwide. Our students acquire advanced teaming skills, appreciate the impact of *management systems*, and understand the strategic and operating applications of new technologies."[6]

Professor Michael Lawson, longest serving associate dean in SMG history

SMG hosts international case competition, 2009. Telecom leader, Ericsson, was an SMG corporate sponsor. Dean Lataif (right) congratulates winning team.

SMG'S RECORD OF ACADEMIC EXCELLENCE: NEW ACHIEVEMENTS, NEW CONFLICTS
Accreditation and Rankings

Academic excellence and high academic standards have been core values throughout the school's history, although reasonable people have differed as to how best to achieve them. The challenges reached back as far as 1921, when CBA raised undergraduate requirements from 120 to 140 credit hours, reportedly the highest level among all colleges of commerce in the United States at the time. The new standards had some unexpected consequences at first: in June 1921, after adding new courses in science, fine arts, mathematics, American government, and modern foreign languages, sixty students were dismissed for failing to pass, equaling 5 percent of all degree candidates.

CELEBRATING TEACHING EXCELLENCE

Metcalf Prize Recipients

In 1974, Arthur G. B. Metcalf, chairman of Boston University's board of trustees, created and endowed the Metcalf Cup and Prize and the Metcalf Awards for Excellence in Teaching. These awards are the university's highest recognition of outstanding teaching-scholars. No more than three Metcalf Prize awards are made annually, and only one nominee from the entire university faculty is named recipient of the Metcalf Cup.

SMG recipients of the Metcalf Cup and Prize are:

1975	Paul Berger	Metcalf Prize (quantitative methods)
1979	George Labovitz	Metcalf Cup and Prize (organizational behavior)
1980	John R. Russell	Metcalf Prize (management policy)
1985	Jules J. Schwartz	Metcalf Prize (management policy)
2007	Jeffrey Beatty	Metcalf Cup and Prize (business law)

Since the 1980s, the School of Management has recognized teaching excellence in the undergraduate and MBA programs by awarding the Broderick Award for Teaching Excellence, named for Richard J. Broderick, Class of '47, who established the gift in 1970.

The Executive MBA (EMBA) program annually awards the John R. Russell Award for Teaching Excellence in Executive Education. The award was endowed by EMBA 7 in thanks for "the extraordinary teaching of Professor Russell," who retired in 1995.

Throughout the school's history, CBA and SMG faculty have taken great pride in the quality of their classroom instruction. Pedagogy changes slowly, but over ten decades formal lectures have given way to case discussions, simulations, field seminars, and other interactive forms of instruction. The faculty has disdained the "one size fits all" instructional model, developing many variations on the basic instructional theme. Within Boston University, SMG has been recognized as a source of excellence in instruction and a number of its faculty members have been recognized as truly elite instructors within the university.

Both SMG and its CBA predecessor also have long histories of honors programs. The 1920s saw the establishment of the first undergraduate honors society, followed by a full-fledged honors program. Although the program was discontinued during World War II, it was eventually resurrected in the 1990s with the support of Provost Dennis Berkey. From there, Assistant Dean Sandra Procopio and faculty members Robert Leone and Michael Salinger led the project further, developing the revived honors program.

In his 2006–7 annual report, in advance of the honors program's tenth year, Dean Lataif discussed efforts to align the interests of very talented students with faculty and several novel program elements. These included a new community service requirement and an International Field Seminar in Ireland that became the capstone of the freshman honors experience.

Another indicator of academic excellence has been BU's long affiliation with Beta Gamma Sigma, the international honor society for business students and faculty. BU's College of Business Administration became an early member of the organization (June 1925), which celebrated its hundredth anniversary in the 2012–13 academic year.[7] The school has also supported Alpha Kappa Psi as an academic honors society. In fact, Everett Lord was an early president of Alpha Kappa Psi and received its first gold medal award on the occasion of this retirement.

But perhaps the most visible expression of SMG's commitment to academic excellence is its participation in the American Association of Collegiate Schools of Business (AACSB). Accreditation by peers became part of business school life when the AACSB was formed in 1916. By 1920, Boston University had joined the association.

AACSB advances business education through an accreditation system based on compliance with standards established by experts in each field. The group conducts a careful review of materials prepared by each school's dean and faculty, followed by a site visit in which a team of deans from peer schools meet face-to-face with administrators, faculty, and students. A formal report and accreditation decision is submitted to the school's dean and president, and when necessary, the AACSB recommends corrective action.

Accreditation is an important asset in the higher education market. Advertisements from as early as the 1920s and 1930s make reference to "AACSB-accredited" programs, emphasizing academic rigor and integrity of members. As the value of accreditation increased, the review process became more rigorous. By the 1960s and 1970s, following the Gordon-Howell (Ford Foundation) Report, accreditation standards were redesigned around how well each institution taught the "common body of knowledge."

But in the view of deans trying to differentiate their programs from competitors, this approach risked homogeneity. Still others felt that their schools could not match the resources of the larger, better-capitalized universities that dominated AACSB meetings and standards committees. The AACSB responded by moving to a new "mission driven" set of criteria wherein each school would articulate its own mission and define how it intended to meet those standards. By the mid-1990s, this new approach found favor at BU—but it also caused unforeseen consequences.

Assistant Dean Procopio, who came to SMG in 1993, recalls that her first AACSB accreditation required "miles and miles of paper" to provide the vast amount of data demanded by the accreditation process. Proper filing was exhausting and sometimes even contentious. For example, the AACSB had a "50/50 rule": no more than half of the undergraduate curriculum could be composed of management courses, while liberal arts courses should fill the other half. Questions arose: where, for example, was Principles of Economics to be counted? At BU, the course was taught in the College of Liberal Arts but listed as a management requirement. SMG argued that it was part of a liberal education and, hence, properly counted as a CLA course. The AACSB was not easily convinced.

A more serious conflict arose involving faculty staffing. BU has long staffed its courses with a combination of full-time and part-time ("adjunct") faculty members. Adjunct faculty are an important teaching resource since many have "real world" experience that complements academically trained faculty. But the AACSB tried to ensure a specific balance of full-time and part-time faculty for both graduate and undergraduate programs, one that challenged BU's numbers. The school objected, emphasizing the need for flexibility. The two bodies finally reached agreement, but not until several years had passed.

Rankings: Management Decisions Within an Imperfect Evaluation System

AACSB accreditation holds great weight in the eyes of peer academics. But for the general public, one of the most recognized markers of academic excellence has become rankings. The ranking of business schools began in the 1990s when two national magazines began comparing universities on various academic quality dimensions. Then rankings evolved into assessments of areas including business and management. The early rankings suffered a variety of technical problems: academics and administrators challenged the accuracy of the criteria, the instruments for measuring performance, and the actual data produced. Still, public interest in rankings continued to climb, and many prospective students and employers began relying heavily on them. By the 2000s, the ranking of business schools had become a demanding, if imperfect, fact of life.

Dean Lataif took a pragmatic view. Cognizant of the very real impact of rankings, he embraced the marketing and communications challenges involved in promoting the work of the school accordingly. In 2003, he set a new priority for SMG: "to reach the next plateau in the perception of applicants, recruiters, students, parents, and alumni, the school must achieve a higher position in the two key business school rankings, namely *U.S. News & World Report* and *Business Week*."[8]

Positive results began to emerge as early as 2005. The School of Management's work to "produce broadly educated leaders with inquiring minds oriented toward building and adding value," noted the 2004–5 annual report, impressed SMG's target ranking bodies:

Among MBA programs, the School is pleased to have been ranked among the top 50 programs by both Business Week *and* U.S. News and World Report *(where the School was among the top 3 in Massachusetts). In January 2005,* The Financial Times *ranked the School 27th among U.S. MBA programs, a 16-place increase over the previous year.*

Reflecting the school's practical approach to working within an imperfect evaluation system, the report continued, "We continue to believe . . . that there is a *significant lag between perception and reality*" in the rankings. Still, the authors wrote,

As we work to further refine our curricula and improve student services at every level, we remain mindful that rankings, particularly U.S. News *and* Business Week, *continue to influence students, recruiters, alumni, and the wider public. Accordingly, the School must maintain its focus on incoming class quality, the effective placement of our graduates, student satisfaction, and our reputation among peers—all critical rankings criteria.*

Hitting the "Top 25" . . .

From 2000 to 2010, BU's undergraduate program ranking by *U.S. News & World Report* varied from forty-eighth place (2004) to thirty-seventh place (2006), but by 2012, *Bloomberg/Business Week* placed the undergraduate program eighteenth overall, twelfth in academic quality, and in the top ten for finance, law, operations, and strategy.

The MBA program's ranking also improved. In 2010, the full-time MBA program moved to #25 in the 2010 *Economist* magazine assessments. Between 2001 and 2010, the program moved into the "top fifty" domestic (U.S.) MBA programs by the *Financial Times*: from #74 in 2002–3 to #34 in 2010–11. In February 2013, new (2012) rankings from *Bloomberg/Business Week* placed the full-time MBA program at #39 (up one place from 2010 when it was ranked #40), #5 in New England, and #28 nationally by recruiters.[9] These same rankings placed the Professional Evening MBA Program (PEMBA) #1 in Boston and #4 in New England. The *Financial Times* 2012 rankings were similar: the full-time MBA program ranked #44 in the United States and #10 globally in e-business.

SMG also ranked highly in health-care management, public and nonprofit management, and information systems, consistently scoring in the "top ten" among competitors. In executive education, the Executive MBA program has consistently placed at or near #1 among New England EMBA programs, and among the top twenty-five nationally.

DEAN LATAIF'S LEGACY

In September 2009, Lou Lataif sent a message to all SMG faculty, staff, and students announcing his retirement in 2010. The timing was calculated so that the university could conduct a search and recruit a successor who could fully engage throughout the long process of the University Capital Campaign, planned for

Dean Lataif at Farewell Reception sponsored by undergraduate students

launch in 2010. The announcement also gave BU time for another crucial endeavor: a huge retirement celebration.

Throughout his tenure as dean, Lou Lataif loved celebrations. They were an opportunity to show off the SMG building, to talk about the new and exciting directions the school was pursuing, and, of course, to play his beloved piano. Lataif and his wife, Najla, hosted more than three hundred events during his tenure to celebrate SMG, and the dean relished the festivities, bestowing gifts and marking special occasions such as the ground breaking (1994) and opening (1996) of the Rafik J. Hariri Building.

The dean was also a master of the "ask!" Donors knew it was coming, and in many ways, they loved it. Lataif courted friends with such unmistakable purpose and passion that some described his efforts as both "relentless" and characterized by his trademark approach of ensuring that each prospective donor would feel like a special part of SMG.

Lataif's retirement in 2010 provided an opportunity for the BU family to express its appreciation for his extraordinary dedication and service to SMG and to Boston University.

President Brown hosted a retirement party in the university's most elaborate setting, the Trustee's Ballroom on the ninth floor of the Hariri Building. The Lataifs were joined by their children and grandchildren, plus hundreds of friends, colleagues, and admirers. Musical entertainment accompanied dinner, followed by remarks from Chancellor Emeritus John Silber, who quipped that he would not have allowed Lataif to retire if he was still president. President Brown spoke next, and lauded Lataif's lasting impact on Boston University.

Within SMG, a farewell reception for the dean drew a large crowd of faculty and staff members. Many SMG leaders with whom Lataif worked contributed letters of appreciation to the creation of a commemorative book. The introduction, written by Senior Associate Dean Michael Lawson, stressed the difference between change and *transformational* change. Lataif, he emphasized, was unquestionably a transformational leader:

> *Many things can change, yet leave an organization fundamentally the same. Transformation, however, is different. When the building was in transformation, everything changed. When the students*

were in transformation, all other aspects of the School needed to change—processes, placement, admissions, the curriculum, and all of our expectations of one another. When the faculty changed, curricula became more rigorous, and research productivity and its impact improved. When our programs changed, our students changed, as did our faculty requirements. When the staff changed, professionalism increased, processes changed, and efficiency improved. Transformation is comprehensive.[10]

Dean Lataif's legacy also includes the nine endowed professorships created during his deanship, more than any other school at BU. The school also acquired financial resources to provide junior faculty with summer support and to reduce teaching loads, enabling it to better compete against top schools for talented faculty. By the time Dean Lataif retired in 2010, eighty-eight of SMG's 119 faculty had been hired during his tenure. They are part of his legacy. So too are the thousands of students who passed through SMG both before and after the new building was completed. It is no exaggeration to say that Dean Lataif stands alongside Everett W. Lord as two leaders whose ambitions for Boston University were matched only by their talent for inspiring future generations to dream "bold dreams" for their alma mater.

Still, as the first decade of the second millennium came to a close, the search for the next leader of Boston University School of Management was under way.

NOTES

1. Richard Taffe, BU Public Relations Office, June 6, 2013; Rich Barlow, "Remembering 9/11", *BU Today*, September 9, 2011, www.bu.edu/today/2011/remembering-911/.

2. *SMG Annual Reports*, 2001–2004.

3. 406 freshmen entered SMG in Fall 2002, the largest class on record, a 29 percent increase over Fall 2001. 315 freshmen entered in Fall 2003; 375 freshmen entered in the Fall 2004 (second largest class on record at the time). Enrollment continued at these levels throughout the rest of the decade: Fall '07: 383; Fall '08: 372; Fall '09: 349; Fall '10: 397.

4. *SMG Annual Report*, 2002–03 (Boston: Boston University), 1.

5. *SMG Annual Report*, 2006–07 (Boston: Boston University), 1–2.

6. *SMG Annual Report*, 2006–07 (Boston: Boston University), 1. Italics in the original.

7. Boston University's College of Business Administration became a member of the national honor society, Beta Gamma Sigma, on June 5, 1925. The chapter inducts undergraduate and graduate students who have met high academic and community service standards. Membership date confirmed by Debra Binek, Associate Chapter Operations, Beta Gamma Sigma, Inc., February 8, 2013: "The Boston University Beta Gamma Sigma chapter was established on 6/5/1925."

8. *SMG Annual Report, 2002–03* (Boston: Boston University), 1.

9. Interestingly, the full-time MBA was ranked higher by recruiters (#28) than by students (#41).

10. Michael Lawson, "Introduction," *Transformational Leadership: A Celebration of Louis E. Lataif*, May 13, 2010, 3.

CHAPTER SIX
TOWARD THE SECOND CENTURY

A New Leader

The search for **SMG**'s next dean took place amid high expectations and lively conversation about the qualities most prized in a new leader.

The search committee was chaired by Professor N. Venkatraman of the SMG Information Systems Department and included students, faculty, alumni, and administrators, as well as a professional search firm, which enabled the university to consider candidates from many backgrounds.

The Debate Over Leadership Qualities

One fundamental question was, "what key qualities should the search committee prioritize?" Some stressed the candidate's academic administrative experience. Others, particularly faculty, believed that prior academic leadership was an important criterion, especially as the school sought to improve its research reputation. Still others emphasized more abstract qualities, such as the ability to communicate the school's message to donors and other key constituencies. President Brown pointed out that the dean would also have an important role in the university's Capital Campaign, and thus would need the qualities to succeed in this endeavor.

In June 2010, the final selection was made public: President Brown introduced Kenneth Freeman as the Allen Questrom Professor and

Kenneth W. Freeman, Allen Questrom Professor and Dean

Dean of the School of Management. A graduate of Bucknell University, Ken, as he likes to be called, subsequently earned his MBA with high distinction from Harvard Business School.

Freeman's career began at Corning Inc., where he started in financial accounting. In time, he successfully turned around a failing business, designed a spin-off, and was named CEO of this new company, Quest Diagnostics Inc., a medical diagnostic testing services firm. After serving as the company's corporate controller for several years he became a general manager, focused on improving troubled businesses. In 1995 he assumed responsibility for Corning's medical diagnostic testing services business, which he led through its spin-off from Corning as Quest Diagnostics, and subsequent dramatic turnaround and growth. After retiring from Quest Diagnostics, he pursued business from a different angle, joining KKR, a leading private equity firm and serving as a partner. In 2010 (and again in 2013), the *Harvard Business Review* named Ken one of the 100 best-performing CEOs in the world. In 2010, the *Harvard Business Review*, looking back on Freeman's tenure at Quest, named him among the world's Top 100 in its scorecard of best-performing CEOs.[1]

But by the time he came to SMG, Freeman was also no stranger to the issues and challenges facing academia. He had served as a member and then chair of Bucknell's board of trustees, as well as an executive-in-residence at Columbia Business School. Search committee members lauded both his clear understanding of Boston University's challenges and the issues facing management education in the twenty-first century, as well as his vision for how to manage at the intersection of the two.

THE FREEMAN ERA AND THE SHAPE OF THE SCHOOL IN ITS SECOND CENTURY

As Freeman assumed the deanship, a new and crucial leadership quality emerged: his commitment to attentive listening, actively engaging each speaker, and probing deeply to better understand the issues and SMG's culture. The results became evident shortly after his arrival. Beginning in August 2010, he visited with more than one hundred faculty members and dozens of staff members to better understand the school and its needs, as well as the people who composed its community. He shaped each conversation as an invitation to share facts, interpretations, and opinions about all aspects of life at SMG. Not surprisingly, he emerged with a long list of issues and suggestions, providing

Dean Ken Freeman

him ample material and information about where and how the school could grow.

He followed this "listening phase" with a planning process, enabling the school to shape a set of priorities relevant to its strengths and gaps, as well as to the broader business and leadership landscape in which SMG functions. Faculty task forces were convened to help focus the school's direction and opportunities in key areas: information technology, health, sustainability, globalization, and finance. Broadening the conversation to include a wide swath of the faculty community, the task forces prepared background reports and discussed

them with the dean and their colleagues at a one-day faculty retreat. In a highly interactive process, more than one hundred faculty members engaged in the effort to identify, frame, and prioritize the school's most pressing needs, meeting in groups to critique ideas, refine recommendations, and solidify priorities.

Then Freeman convened a set of task forces to address six action areas around the priorities already identified: undergraduate curricula, graduate curricula, research infrastructure, globalization of management education, ethics and social responsibility, and executive education. Finally, the school's new direction and shape for its second century emerged. The dean's first annual report highlighted its most crucial growth areas and the actions necessary to foster them:[2]

1. Update/revise curricula in both the undergraduate and MBA programs.
2. Emphasize and further develop the school's strengths in health, digital technology, and sustainability.
3. Develop key learning themes related to globalization, ethics, and social responsibility across the undergraduate and graduate curricula.
4. Improve SMG's research infrastructure.
5. Raise the school's profile and position in published rankings.

Valuing Both the Product and the Process

The school's future success will likely be measured in terms of how well the initiatives above can be executed. All have begun to be implemented, and changes such as a revised undergraduate and MBA curricula will go into effect at the start of the 2013–14 academic year. But beneath these operational goals lies a deeper set of aspirations, one that springs from Dean Freeman's leadership values. The process, as well as the product, matters greatly to him. By investing significant time in listening to each faculty member's views of the school, its strengths, and its issues, and by ensuring that everyone be invited to contribute to defining a "top tier" of issues and actions, Freeman has produced high buy-in. In an interview for this book, he commented: "It's all about the people," and added, "it's not my strategy; its 'ours.' . . . We own it together and will achieve it together."

Freeman sent another strong signal when he moved his office from the traditional dean's fifth

Allen Questrom, Class of '64, University Trustee and SMG benefactor. Among Mr. Questrom's generous gifts to SMG is his endowment of the Allen Questrom Professor and Dean chair in 2010.

floor suite to a second-floor, glass-walled office in order to be closer to students and to maintain a visible presence throughout SMG. Academic leadership is similar to business leadership in many ways: people want to achieve something important, something that reflects their values, and believe that their efforts are respected. Culture matters.

Physical Expansion

Once again, new growth areas have created the need for SMG to adapt and expand its existing physical space. During the summers of 2012 and 2013, construction took place within the Hariri Building to add new offices and classrooms. In the planning stage is an addition to "595," including a connection to a new building facing Bay State Road. A generous gift by alumnus Allen Questrom[3] and his wife, Kelli, has enabled architectural planning to move forward as the SMG Centennial unfolds.

Building the Research Enterprise

Improving the quantity and impact of faculty research is an imperative within SMG and the university. President Brown is publicly committed

to solidifying BU's position as a top tier research institution and has created a research infrastructure to support expanded grant and contract activity. The growing emphasis on both research and teaching is demonstrated through the recognition of a growing number of senior faculty holding endowed professorships [See Boxed Insert] and those designated as Everett W. Lord Scholars.

SMG has traditionally directed its research toward business policy and practice, but is now being called on to collaborate with other BU units in cross-disciplinary projects and institutes in areas such as financial policy, health-care delivery, and sustainable communities. Under the direction of Senior Associate Dean Karen Golden-Biddle, a full review of SMG research activity and infrastructure is under way and innovations such as an annual Research Day have been launched to further showcase faculty research projects.

THE SECOND CENTURY: ENDURING THEMES

As it begins its second century, Boston University School of Management is well prepared to face the challenges ahead. SMG

CHAIRED PROFESSORS, CIRCA 2013

The School of Management has ten chaired professors. Endowed professorships support the resarch and innovative activities of the named professor. Each professor is a leader in his or her field, as well as a leader within the School and University.

 Kenneth W. Freeman, Allen Questrom Professor and Dean in Management

 Zvi Bodie, Norman & Adele Barron Professor in Management

 Iain M. Cockburn, Richard C. Shipley Professor in Management

 Douglas T. Hall, Morton H. & Charlotte Friedman Professor in Management

 Kathy E. Kram, Richard C. Shipley Professor in Management

 Nalin H. Kulatilaka, Wing Tat Lee Family Professor in Management

 James E. Post, John F. Smith, Jr. Professor in Management

 Michael A. Salinger, Jacqueline J. & Arthur S. Bahr Professor in Management

 Michael Shwartz, Richard D. Cohen Professor in Management

 N. Venkatraman, David J. McGrath, Jr. Professor in Management

represents a vision of creating value for the world, an entrepreneurial spirit that drives innovation, and an expanding infrastructure of people, programs, and resources that will enable its deans, faculty, and professional staff to serve and encourage those who study here to continue to "dream big."

As we look to SMG's next century, several themes stand out that frame the story of the school's first one hundred years and remain relevant at the cusp of its second.

1. An Entrepreneurial Spirit

Throughout its history Boston University has been an entrepreneurial enterprise. Blessed with neither the vast endowment nor the commercialized technology base of its two Charles River neighbors, BU has operated a lean, yet creative, enterprise throughout its first century. This has encouraged faculty members to be imaginative and to create new programs that meet market needs. The school's executive education program continues a long tradition of developing innovative courses, workshops, and research for companies and other client organizations, enhancing both SMG's revenues and its reputation.

SMG's large enrollment, and its careful husbanding of resources, has enabled it to support a few ventures that do not typically generate surplus funds but serve a larger mission. Doctoral education, for example, has been part of the SMG research commitment since the early 1980s; the program now offers PhD degrees in management and mathematical finance and is becoming an integral element of the school's research enterprise. And its graduates are sought after by other leading management schools.

The school has demonstrated self-reliance and tenacity that have helped it adapt to the market challenges of a changing world. Some of its ventures have grown to become academic and commercial successes in other parts of Boston University. During World War I, for example, CBA offered courses in the "secretarial and commercial sciences," which were highly favored as preparation to become secretaries and high school teachers of bookkeeping, secretarial science, and administration.[4] After the war, the demand was so great that this initiative became a new college, called the College of Practical Arts and Letters (PAL), which was led for decades by Dean T. Lawrence Davis, CBA's first graduate (1915).

Forty years ago, in the 1970s, the idea of service to society led SMG to create the Health Care Management and Public and Nonprofit Management programs within its graduate MBA offerings. These programs continue to make distinctive contributions to the community as well as to the health-care, public, and nonprofit management professions. Graduates of these programs are found throughout New England's health sector and public and nonprofit management ranks.

Another distinctive initiative is the MS•MBA program, a dual degree master's program, now in its second decade. Graduates develop a special competence in the application of technology for operating and strategic advantage. As digital technology transforms industry after industry, the school is preparing a new generation of technology-wise leaders.

There is little doubt that the school will continue to incubate such new ventures in its degree and executive education programs, as well as online settings. This entrepreneurial spirit will surely lead to a multitude of exciting new endeavors in the school's second century.

2. The Cultural and the Practical: Creating Value for the World

From its earliest days, Boston University has emphasized the importance of cultivating an understanding of the larger society in which we live while also developing the practical skills of business and management. On October 13, 1913, the day the business program opened, three classes met: English, Spanish, and Advertising. Today, those classes are taught elsewhere within BU (CAS and COM) while more specialized courses are taught through SMG. Together, they form the kind of education Everett Lord believed in: "Culture and skill are not only compatible, but the truest culture comes only in combination with skill." (Brass plate on E. W. Lord's portrait) All SMG undergraduate students leave with business skills deeply contextualized within the framework of a liberal education; graduate students leave with deep specialized knowledge, but always in the context of a changing society. The modern curriculum continues to balance the "cultural" with the "practical" in ways that Dean Lord and his successors would recognize and likely applaud.

Today's students know that their skills and competencies must be accompanied by an informed perspective on how economics, culture, and society function and interact in the modern world. This view is fostered through courses, team projects, and travel experiences. One third of SMG undergraduates now complete a study abroad program before graduating, and the trend is upward. Understanding the global cultural context in which business operates is crucial to a liberal education. Curriculum remains a focus of faculty attention, and both the undergraduate and graduate programs struggle to balance specialized elective courses with a core curriculum that every student must master. As the new undergraduate and MBA curricula show, the faculty in SMG's eight academic departments—Accounting, Economics (Markets, Public Policy, & Law), Finance, Information Systems, Marketing, Operations Management & Technology, Organizational Behavior, and Strategy & Innovation—are constantly reinventing ways to deliver core content more effectively and efficiently.

When the College of Business Administration was founded in 1913, Frederick Taylor's theory of "scientific management" was new and modern. Principles of accounting, economics, and managing people were just beginning to emerge in twentieth-century form. But in the

course of a century, both the content and the process of teaching how to more effectively manage money, information, and people have been transformed. At its core, management education is the never-ending challenge of training today's men and women to be agents of change, able to improve all of the institutions that serve society.

3. Ethics, Professionalism, and Service to Society

Generations of women and men have brought their personal values and experience to the school, engaged with others, and then taken their new knowledge and personal integrity into the world. Honesty, truthfulness, and respect have been foundational values throughout SMG's history. Economic and social events have repeatedly confirmed what deans and faculty have long argued: that ethics and professionalism should play a central role in any curriculum shaping future leaders.

In 1926, Everett W. Lord published *Fundamentals of Business Ethics*,[5] wherein he offered this simple and enduring counsel: ethics is the "science of conduct," the study of the right and the wrong, the good and the bad, the moral and the immoral. "Right," "good," and "moral" are not synonymous, he noted. But our job—as students, managers, educators—is to recognize where these ideas overlap and where they either reinforce or conflict with one another, and then use logic and "science" to create the best outcome.

Lord's pragmatic philosophy permeated business education at BU until World War II but suffered as the pressure for "trade school" courses intensified through the 1950s. It took more than a decade after the Gordon-Howell critique of business education was published in 1959 for business schools, including CBA, to refocus on professional ethics and business responsibility to society. One of Dean Peter Gabriel's initiatives in 1973 was to create a required freshman course called Management in Society; a comparable course was then designed for the MBA program. Today, new efforts are under way to integrate ethics and professionalism throughout the undergraduate and MBA programs, beginning with a new freshman course, Business, Society, and Ethics, and a graduate offering, Ethics, Values and Responsibility.

SMG student volunteers celebrate a community service day, circa 2005.

Nautical seal located in the lobby of the Charles Hayden Memorial, 685 Commonwealth Avenue. This seal was designed by Dean Lord and is reminiscent of the sailing ships his father captained. Note that the ship is headed "Down East."

In 1913, the CBA was formed, in part, to promote professional standards of business practice and to help drive out the trade school charlatans that were fostering unethical and illegal practices. This was the foundation of the view that the purpose of a business education was "service to society." Through its history, CBA/SMG has developed high standards of professional practice, encouraged and supported professional societies and fraternities, and promoted the concept of professionalism in management in service to society. This commitment to professionalism has become a signature feature of the BU brand as faculty, staff, and students continuously work toward the ideal of knowledge with integrity.

4. Community: From Local to Global

Many students come to BU excited to experience life in Boston, a city of enormous intellectual and social appeal. They soon discover that it is a city with a heart as well as a head. For all its intellectual resources, Boston's spirit of community provides an extra dimension to student life here. BU plays a big role in the life of the city, and SMG plays a big role within BU.

Undergraduates are drawn into a wide range of initiatives that support community organizations, raise funds for charities, and link the city to the university. Undergraduate experiences such as the honors program offer a built-in service component, and the alumni of many graduate programs, including health-care management and public and nonprofit management, play leadership roles in community organizations throughout Boston.

SMG also works hard to foster its own particular community ethos: faculty, students, and staff share a passion for their fields and support one another in their professional development

through clubs and career networks while at BU and beyond. Perhaps at no other school within the university is the concept of teaming—of learning within and growing alongside—a community so prevalent. This idea of "community within community" also connects graduates of decades past with the graduates of today. This culture is especially strong among students and graduates in various cohorts and specializations.

The "power of community" reached new heights in the aftermath of the 2013 Boston Marathon bombing. One Boston University student died and several others were among the injured, but BU students and staff members were also among the many volunteers who have made "Boston Strong" a recognizable message around the world.

As SMG moves into its second century, both Boston University and the School of Management can feel pride that they are recognized—and valued—around the world. Under the leadership of President Robert Brown, BU has developed a plan to guide the university's global engagement for decades to come. SMG Dean Ken Freeman has spent considerable time in Asia and Europe, two prime regions for expanded activities. With 33 percent of SMG graduates having participated in the university's study abroad programs in 2012, a trend that is increasing, and with international field seminars becoming a vital component of MBA education, a global perspective is becoming another signature theme of a twenty-first-century BU education.

Globalization is more than recruiting students or offering courses in foreign locations: it is a world-view and a state of mind. It is the recognition that people are interdependent, that governments must work together to combat common threats such as climate change, and that commerce in all its varied forms requires, and contributes to, peaceful relations among all people.

Everett W. Lord would appreciate BU's educational commitment to the global community. Just as he considered culture and skill to be integral to one's education, he saw the "global" and the "local" as elements of a coherent worldview. In fact, only two years after founding a full-time program in Boston, he established a business program and presence in Havana, Cuba, selling guarantee bonds to Cuban businessmen to underwrite a business program. Only the collapse of the sugar market in 1920 prevented BU from having a Havana campus by the 1920s.[6] New initiatives followed, with greater success in Puerto Rico, and it was

Lord's idea to create the nautical seal of a sailing ship in the entrance to the Charles Hayden Memorial. Today, SMG has global learning initiatives in China, Japan, and dozens of study abroad locations, a commitment symbolized in Sergio Castillo's sculpture *Earth Orbit*, located in the atrium of "595". Today, modern technology has further promoted global thinking and provided a new means for responding to world issues. SMG's recently organized office of global initiatives is poised to advance this agenda.

THE DEAN'S MESSAGE

Ken Freeman has refined his message over the course of three years, using his introductory "Letter from the Dean" in each issue of the school's magazine to highlight central themes. These letters describe the change that has taken place since his arrival, beginning with "A New Beginning" (Fall 2010), "Creating Value for the World" (Winter 2012), and "Transformation" (Summer 2012).[7] In his letter for the Spring 2013 magazine, Freeman summarized two lessons he has learned during his three years as dean: "Change is our constant companion at the School of Management. . . . We didn't get to be a century old by playing it safe."

Commencement 2013

On May 17, 2013, Dean Ken Freeman called more than 620 undergraduate students and several thousand family members and friends to order in the Agganis Arena for the School of Management commencement ceremony. The crowd was ready to celebrate the joyous ritual of achievement and

passage as Dean Freeman began:

Welcome to the undergraduate honors and diploma convocation of the School of Management in the one hundredth year of the one hundred and seventy-fourth year of Boston University, and in particular, welcome to the Class of 2013!!"[8]

Commencement—celebrating achievement, anticipating great things

On the stage, looking out at hundreds of scarlet-robed graduates, dozens of SMG professors, in their own multicolored academic robes, admired these students who had mastered the curriculum, created a personal career plan, and stood ready to leave BU for a world of opportunity and challenge.

Commencement is an end but also a beginning. Once again, events reminded us that the histories of institutions begin with stories of individuals. In a university, the "story" gets richer with each generation of students, faculty, administrators, and families. At Boston University, the story of the School of Management has changed, deepened, and become more diverse and exciting over one hundred years, truly a century of change.

Graduations are a time of speeches and lofty thoughts. More than most, this commencement was a time for such reflections, following as it did on the Boston Marathon bombings and the deaths over the year of a number of members of the class of 2013.

At the baccalaureate service in Marsh Chapel, held shortly before the all-university event, Dr. Peter Weaver, a Methodist bishop and former BU trustee, spoke of "dreaming with eyes wide open." Commencement is the culmination of old dreams and the opening of new dreams, he argued, and dreams are "the incarnation of imagination." That is why we always need to have a "next dream." Throughout the history of Boston University, this notion of dreams nurturing action has been our institutional DNA.

For one hundred years, the story of the School of Management has involved "dreaming, nurturing, and action." The school has nurtured the dreams of thousands of students over the past century, and proudly watched as those dreams became reality. From T. Lawrence Davis, the first graduate of the College of Business Administration in 1915, to the graduates of 2013, and all those yet to come, BU alumni and students are making a difference as they create value for the world.

That is the promise of a great university, an institution that grows stronger and better as it creates meaning through the stories of individuals: students, alumni, faculty, staff, donors, and friends. The global accreditation organization AACSB articulates the goal this way: "Quality business schools have legacies of achievement, improvement, and impact." Against this standard, Boston University's School of Management stands tall.

NOTES

1. "Dean Freeman Named a Top 100 CEO by HBR," *Boston University School of Management*, January 22, 2013, http://management.bu.edu/blog/2013/01/22/dean-freeman-named-a-top-100-ceo-by-hbr/.

2. *SMG Annual Report, 2010–11* (Boston: Boston University).

3. "SMG Receives $10 Million Gift," *BU Today*, May 17, 2012. "I wouldn't have found a fitting career in retailing without BU, so I have a very clear responsibility to give back," says Questrom. The first in his family to attend a university, he studied finance and marketing, but had "no idea" what he wanted to do until he excelled in an elective course in retailing. He says his marketing professor, A. E. Beckwith, "was very instrumental in pushing me to attend a particular retail interview, and when I did I was attracted to the company for its great training program." His SMG course work gave him a substantial academic edge, adds Questrom, who took the job and went on to legendary success, restoring to health several retail corporations, saving and creating thousands of jobs, and himself ranking in the Forbes list of highest paid executives for several years running. "I probably wouldn't have qualified for that first job if I hadn't gone to BU," he says, "so I want BU and SMG to be a priority in my charitable interests." www.bu.edu/today/2012/smg-receives-10-million-gift/

4. Kilgore, *Transformations*, 408.

5. Everett W. Lord, *Fundamentals of Business Ethics* (New York: Ronald Press, 1926), 14–15.

6. Kilgore, *Transformations*, 130, has a colorful account of BU's Havana initiative. Havana's reputation for gambling, prostitution, and open drinking clashed with the university's Methodist heritage and prompted criticism from many quarters. Note, as well, that this initiative took place when Prohibition was in effect in the United States.

7. "The 97th academic year in the history of Boston University School of Management is underway. Your School is a buzz of activity on many fronts . . . It is a privilege and an honor to serve as your new dean. I look forward to building on (Lou Lataif's) legacy as we continue the pursuit of greatness . . . The opportunity is clear: to create value in a changing world." (Kenneth Freeman, "A New Beginning," *Builders & Leaders*, Fall 2010); "Boston University School of Management is in the midst of a remarkable transformation. During a time of tremendous global economic and political uncertainty, we have developed a compelling strategic vision (of Creating Value for the World.) We will distinguish ourselves by focusing on the facets of value creation, from financial to societal." (Kenneth Freeman, "Creating Value for the World," *Builders & Leaders*, Winter 2012); "Remarkable things are happening at Boston University School of Management. We are in the midst of transforming the School into one of the world's elite business schools, building on the strong foundation created over almost twenty years by Dean Emeritus Lou Lataif and the broad SMG community. . . . Our second century is rapidly approaching, with celebrations to begin in September 2013 as we bring the strategic vision of 'Creating Value for the World' to life." (Kenneth Freeman, "Transformation," *Builders & Leaders*, Summer 2012.)

8. Thanks to Erik Linnane, Undergraduate Program Office, for providing the original text.

TIMELINE

1913 First business classes offered, October 13, 1913; College of Business Administration (CBA) is established

1916 Full time program (Day Division) approved; CBA to offer bachelors and masters degree programs

1926 Everett W. Lord publishes *Fundamentals of Business Ethics* (New York: Ronald Press)

1938 Ground broken for the first building on the Charles River campus

1939 Dedication of Charles Hayden Memorial as home of the College of Business Administration

1941 Everett W. Lord retires at age 70

1941 William Sutcliffe named second dean of CBA

1941 World War II begins

1958 Dean Sutcliffe retires; Philip Ragan named the third Dean of CBA

1962 James W. Kelley named Dean, *ad interim*

1963 John F. Fielden named Dean

1971 Arthur Thompson named Dean, *ad interim*

1973 Peter P. Gabriel named Dean

1974 CBA is renamed SMG

1976 Peter Gabriel resigns; David Furer named Dean, *ad interim*

1977 Jules J. Schwartz named Dean

1979 Henry M. Morgan named Dean

1986 George W. McGurn named Dean

1991 Douglas T. Hall named Dean, *ad interim*

1991 Louis E. Lataif named Dean

1994 Ground broken for Rafik B. Hariri Building

1996 SMG occupies new home at 595 Commonwealth Avenue

2002 MS•MBA joint degree program offered

2009 Dean Lataif announces intention to retire (Sept 2009)

2010 Kenneth W. Freeman named Dean

2013 100th anniversary of CBA/SMG as a unit of Boston University

Commonwealth Avenue and College of Business Administration, looking east, 1957. The College inhabited 685 Commonwealth Avenue for over fifty years.

ACKNOWLEDGMENTS

This book is the product of conversations and collaboration with many past and current faculty colleagues, members of SMG's professional staff, and a dedicated research team who tracked down facts, photos, and memorabilia. Happily, the longer we worked on the project, the more interesting and illuminating our discoveries.

The early history of the School is based on documents, artifacts, and a handful of newspaper articles and published interviews with the pioneers who led the College of Business Administration in its early decades. Two legendary figures of this era are founding Dean Everett W. Lord, whose papers in the Gottlieb Archive are of great value, and whose story is central to the first half of SMG's history, and Professor Raymond Mannix, whose life story is also astounding: He graduated from CBA in 1923 (BBA) and 1924 (MBA), taught accounting and chaired the department from 1924 to 1968, and actively participated in SMG affairs well into his nineties, when he attended

the dedication of the Hariri Building in 1994. These records of dedication and loyal service shaped the School's early history and culture.

The second half of the historical story is based on eyewitness accounts, as well as a more extensive collection of documents and memorabilia. Throughout this process, I was fortunate to interview a number of retired faculty members and students who were active amidst the tumult of the late 1960s and 1970s. Among the important developments that took place in the 1970s was the arrival of the "Class of '74," a dozen or so faculty members, many of whom would play important roles in the School over the next thirty years. I am grateful for their patience and cooperation as we reconstructed some of the signal events of the 1980s, 1990s, and beyond. I am also appreciative of the interest, humor, and patience of current colleagues who have encouraged this effort. Perhaps they will better understand SMG's first century as they shape and define their own roles in the story of the school's second century.

I am indebted to Tracy L. Slater, whose editing made this book more readable and interesting. I am grateful to Dean Ken Freeman, who provided encouragement throughout; Midge Wilcke, who sponsored this book as one of SMG's centennial projects; Joshua Stevens and Matthew Heidenry of Reedy Press, who guided the publication process from document to publication; and a host of supporters, beginning with my wife, Jeannette, and a circle of readers, critics, and friends including Ken Hatten, Michael Lawson, and Sandra Procopio, who generously shared their time and counsel.

The impossibility of listing the names of everyone who contributed to this book does not lessen the need to acknowledge the contributions of several people without whose assistance this project would never have become reality. Arlyne Jackson, Head of the Frederick S. Pardee Management Library, provided important guidance that opened the doors to Everett Lord's story and the public record of SMG deans from Peter Gabriel to Louis E. Lataif; former Senior Associate Deans Edwin A. Murray, Jr. and Michael Lawson provided administrative perspectives on the past thirty-five years; Professors Fred Foulkes, Jeffrey Miller, George Labovitz, Ken Hatten, and Assistant Deans Sandra Procopio, Kathie Nolan, and Steve Davidson shed light on important academic and administrative initiatives of recent decades; Mary Sforza, who organized a long list of memorable social and business events from 1996 to the present, and generously shared her recollections and insights; and Greg DeFronzo, director of SMG's technology services, who occupied the office next to mine, provided unfailing good cheer during our many hallway conversations. Of special note, the photo research that enlivens the entire SMG narrative is attributable to the extraordinary skills of Adriane Dean, Midge Wilcke, Megan Doiron, and student researchers Sean Flaherty and Peter Egan. Heartfelt thanks to all for your contributions.

Finally, a special word of thanks to Jack Smith, a distinguished graduate of SMG, who endowed the John F. Smith, Jr. Professorship that supported research for this project.

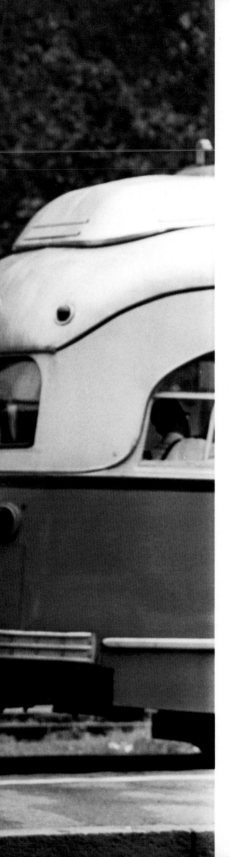

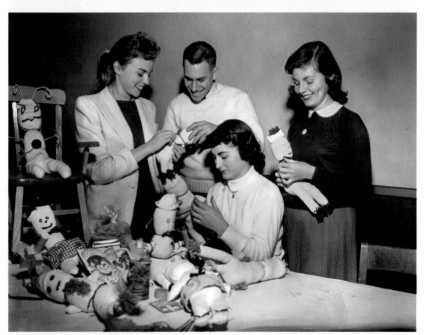

Facing: **MBTA Green Line** has always provided easy access to SMG, 1966.

Facing/Inset: Wayfinding signage for SMG, 2012

Top: CBA Dean's Reception; future dean Louis E. Lataif in foreground, 1958

Bottom: Student volunteers, holiday toy drive, late 1950s

Facing top left: Entrance to CBA at 685 Commonwealth Avenue

Facing top right: A faculty member and student work on a slim-fitting IBM computer, 1961.

Facing bottom: CBA fraternity social, 1952

Top: Evening class in session, circa 1969

Right: Final exams in Hayden Memorial

Rafik B. Hariri Building
clockwise from top left: Construction at 595 Commonwealth Avenue, circa 1994; Professor Paul Carlisle teaching Information Systems class, circa 2012; Celebration luncheon in the new atrium following the "topping off" ceremonies, 1995; Study carrels in Frederick Pardee Library.

Spiral staircase
in the Frederick
Pardee Library

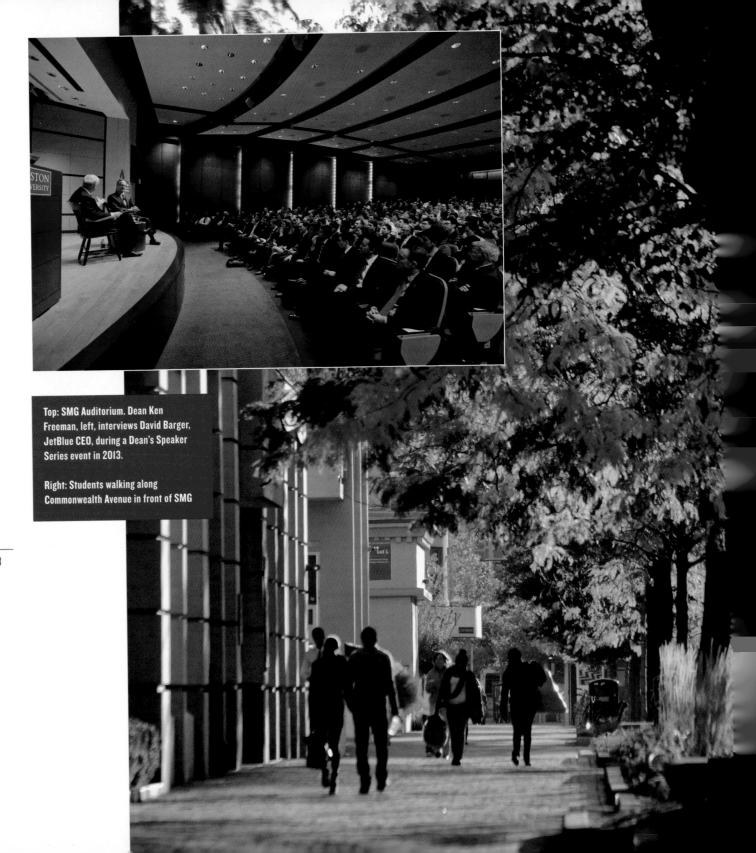

Top: SMG Auditorium. Dean Ken Freeman, left, interviews David Barger, JetBlue CEO, during a Dean's Speaker Series event in 2013.

Right: Students walking along Commonwealth Avenue in front of SMG

INDEX